PRAISE FOR GOOD
IN TURBULENT TIMES

I'm so glad that my mother 'jauntily suggested' that Martin and his family go white water rafting. Little did she know at the time what a vivid analogy for navigating turbulent times it would turn out to be!

Good Leaders in Turbulent Times is an easy-to-read, insightful and empowering book that will help guide any good leader seeking to be significant in this topsy-turvy world.

Martin weaves his wealth of experience as a facilitator with deep empathy and kindness to create a valuable book for those of us navigating the wild waters of work.

Having personally experienced the challenges of navigating Covid-19 as an international travel business whilst trying to meet some of the needs of vulnerable children in a country with the highest HIV infection rate in the world and 60% of people living in poverty, I'm very grateful for Martin's reassuring and encouraging insights.
KIM ROQUES, FOUNDER & DIRECTOR, ALL OUT AFRICA, ESWATINI

This book is packed with truths – some of them a little uncomfortable to face, but all of them invaluable for anyone trying to navigate the wild waters of civil society leadership. Whether you are a novice CEO in your first role or a long-in-the-tooth leader who has been round the block several times, you'll find thought provoking and actionable content here that can help you avoid landing on the rocks hidden beneath the waves.

I suspect this is a book I'll keep coming back to to help me in my own leadership practice, and each time will find something new and invaluable in its pages.

JANE IDE OBE HON D UNIV, CEO ASSOCIATION OF CHIEF EXECUTIVES OF VOLUNTARY ORGANISATIONS (ACEVO)

To be a leader in civil society is an amazing, rewarding experience but most of us find ourselves battling to keep our heads above water at some point. At such times it can feel catastrophic and very lonely.

Martin takes a wise and compassionate look at living through leadership crises and difficult relationships and moving from surviving to thriving. Martin introduces us to a cast of characters who are navigating such wild waters. Through their experiences, he offers insights to help us reflect on and make sense of such difficult times, and offers ways to find healing, learning and growth.

ROS OAKLEY, CO-FOUNDER AND FIRST CHIEF EXECUTIVE, ASSOCIATION OF CHAIRS

Good Leaders in Turbulent Times has come at a time when leadership responsibility for psychological safety, bullying, harassment and well-being of staff and mental *wealth* is so alive! Navigating in a post-Covid environment where there are additional challenges, additional trauma impacts such as matters of inclusion and belonging, generational diversity, artificial intelligence and conflict, to name a few, presents a deep and broad slate for today's leaders.

Focusing on the future with an eye on today, while learning lessons from the past, has never been more important. Martin Farrell has written a really important book.

TESSE AKPEKI, FELLOW OF THE CHARTERED GOVERNANCE INSTITUTE (UK AND IRELAND), CGI CHAMPION FOR GOVERNANCE FOR UK AND IRELAND 2023

Good Leaders in Turbulent Times tells us various tales of third sector 'Good Leaders', who find themselves in a career crisis. It follows them from the first 'watch-out-for' signs, through the bad times and, eventually, we see the resolutions they find. These stories are intertwined with the stories of personal crises that flow alongside the events in their professional lives.

Happily, with Martin guiding us through each twist and turn of their wild waters experiences, sharing his ability to see the full story and with his insights and commentary peppered throughout each chapter, the book is an uplifting and positive read. It will likely help not only those finding themselves in crisis to better navigate their own situation towards a positive end, but may indeed help all leaders avoid getting into wild waters in the first place.
JESPER CHRISTENSEN, PARTNER, MCCARTHY DENNING

This is an energising and liberating book, distilling Martin's decades of experience and insights into how charity leaders can get stuck in the mire of dysfunctional dynamics such as 'them and us' and consequently find themselves being battered in wild waters.

It shines a light on stories (usually never told) of the conflicts and personal trauma and offers clear advice for navigating a way through crises with integrity, honesty and compassion – and how to emerge stronger.

It is full of practical advice for leaders about recognizing the early red flags in the boardroom, taking prompt action and building more effective and more equitable Chair/CEO relationships.

Good Leaders in Turbulent Times is essential reading for all chairs and chief executives and all who care about charity governance.
JANE KEEPER, SOCIAL WORKER, FORMER DIRECTOR OF OPERATIONS AT REFUGE

I see the bodhisattva in Martin; that is, when he sees suffering and injustice, he responds with compassion and works tirelessly to help others be the best they can be. Martin has an irrepressible love of life that is evident in his vigour, authentic kindness and wit. People feel better when they are around him.

In addition to these powerful personal attributes, Martin has the technical knowledge base and skills needed to guide, support and problem-solve with leaders in complex systems.

The next best thing to being in the room with Martin is reading *Good Leaders in Turbulent Times*. You will find him on every page.
GREG DALDER, SEMI-RETIRED SOCIAL WORKER AND BEREAVEMENT COUNSELLOR, TUCSON, ARIZONA, USA

If you are looking for a leadership guide by your side, go no further. In *Good Leaders in Turbulent Times* Martin speaks personally to every leader about navigating 'wild waters' in our turbulent times; distilled wisdom pours throughout this book.

Each character and Martin's commentary speak to each reader in ways which suit their own situation. No dos and don'ts, just gentle invitations that fall like soft snow, inviting exploration of ideas that help you through. Martin has navigated wild waters, not only for himself, but also for every leader. No Mud, no Lotus. Indeed.
V NARASIMHAN ('NARSI'), CHENNAI, INDIA

Good Leaders in Turbulent Times powerfully brings to mind my work with leaders in civil society – the chaos, bitterness, burnouts, and also the passion, virtues and resilience that flourish amidst adversity. Martin's portrayal of 'wild water experiences' resonates deeply with challenges and opportunities I have seen in my part of the world.

As I immerse myself in the characters' stories, I eagerly anticipate Martin's insights. His parallel commentaries offer precious guidance, which I will carry with me as I facilitate and coach in the years ahead.
LILIAN WANG, CERTIFIED PROFESSIONAL FACILITATOR | MASTER, EXECUTIVE COACH, ASIA PACIFIC

Good Leaders in Turbulent Times by Martin Farrell is a provocative guide for navigating the stormy seas of leadership challenges. With insights drawn from his first-hand years of experience in working with and coaching high-level leaders and CEOs, including for charitable and international organizations, this book equips aspiring leaders with guidance on the wisdom and fortitude needed to thrive amidst uncertainty.

A must-read for anyone seeking to lead with courage, empathy and conviction in today's unpredictable and challenging world.

The daunting task, while taken seriously, is lightened by witty anecdotes, storytelling, familiar day-to-day encounters over coffee and initial reactions to having to sit through 27 slides. Magnified is also the element of self-doubt and the human perspective of feeling alone or having family and friends nudging, to which any reader can undoubtedly relate. You are certainly left with a strong sense that the coach is in the room inside the pages and between the lines.
AMBASSADOR SALWA DALLALAH, MANAGER AND DIRECTOR CONFERENCE AFFAIRS SERVICES UNFCCC 1997–2015 AND IAEA 2016–2020

Martin Farrell brings common sense, emotional intelligence and humanity to *Good Leaders*… In his work and in this book he holds the big picture of the organizational dynamic, whilst taking a deep dive into 'wild waters' with leaders. Everyone emerges the better for it.

It is a rare gift indeed to be exceptional at what you do *and* deftly articulate it, but in this creative and absorbing book Martin does just that.

He rightly has a stellar reputation for supporting CEOs in crisis. The third sector is a better place with Martin in it and *Good Leaders…* will serve to enrich it even further.
AMANDA FALKSON, PSYCHOTHERAPY CITY, LONDON

Martin writes with clarity and knowledge about his approach in this creative fictional story, which is well integrated with solid guiding principles for leaders in crisis.

It is his therapeutic understanding that takes *Good Leaders in Turbulent Times* to a deeper level beyond a technical and prescriptive textbook. His experience enables him to be the 'wise man' and hold the space and make it safe for the drama to unfold, knowing that the client in crisis needs to find the answers from within for change and healing to occur. Martin also invites emotional release for clearer thinking, so emphasizing body awareness and mindfulness as resources to achieve better self-regulation. In so doing he draws attention to unconscious messages.

Despite Martin's wealth of experience, he remains humble with respect to the mutuality of the process and the partnership with his clients. Martin guides with authority and shares his own vulnerability, whilst balancing this with letting the client be in charge of their own process.

The human-ness in his work makes it truly relational. Inviting the reader's full engagement, *Good Leaders in Turbulent Times* avoids being yet another 'tick box' exercise.
BERND EIDEN, MA, CO-FOUNDER AND DIRECTOR OF THE CHIRON CENTRE FOR BODY PSYCHOTHERAPY, 1983–2011.

GOOD LEADERS IN TURBULENT TIMES

How to Navigate
Wild Waters at Work

MARTIN FARRELL

First published in Great Britain by Practical Inspiration Publishing, 2024

ISBN 9781788605526 (hardback)
      9781788605533 (paperback)
      9781788605557 (epub)
      9781788605540 (mobi)

Want to bulk-buy copies of this book for your team and colleagues? We can customize the content and co-brand *Good Leaders in Turbulent Times* to suit your organization's needs.

Please email info@practicalinspiration.com for more details.

for martin...

steven apx 2006

Drawing by Steven Appleby of Martin Farrell on his motorbike.

Drawings by Steven Appleby are reproduced here with his kind permission, their having been first published in Lois Graessle, George Gawlinski *Meeting Together* 2006.

Cover lifering drawing by Steven Appleby specially commissioned for this book.

Cover and page design by Marianne Hartley of Hartley & Soul www.hartleyandsoul.com

Cover photo by Free Nomad on Unsplash.

Cover photo of author by Rachel Youngman.

Photo on p 234 of author with a calligraphy by Thích Nhất Hạnh by Rosanna Farrell.

For my number one collaborator, my wife Korinna,
who is my first and closest supporter and has been the most long-
suffering and sharpest critic of my efforts to find my voice in this
book, over nearly eight years from conception to publication…

… and for all the leaders whom I will never know who,
facing the challenges of turbulent times, are courageously aspiring
to be the good leaders who will sustain a decent, just and civil
society, so we can all live together well for the foreseeable future.

CONTENTS

CONTENTS

PLEASE READ THIS BEFORE YOU DIVE IN

Beware. Some readers may be emotionally triggered by some of what they read in this book; in fact it's quite likely. You may laugh, feel upset or recall painful moments. If you're triggered in any way, please follow the advice in the book, seek help, do not face it alone.

Good Leaders in Turbulent Times: How to Navigate Wild Waters at Work contains stories with characters who are all entirely fictional. This means that any resemblance to any real people, past or present in the UK or elsewhere, is coincidental and unintended.

All the commentary and advice, however, is real.

Steven Appleby's absurdist drawings invite us into a fantastical world that is free of the boundaries of our real-world personal characteristics and they engagingly portray a sense of the turmoil, fear and obsession that teem beneath the exterior of most of us.

Everything I have written, both fictional and real, is intended to be of service to good leaders everywhere.

Martin

HOW TO NAVIGATE THIS BOOK

There are five ways you can safely navigate this book:

1. Read the stories of each of the fictional characters in the first four chapters.
2. Start with contributions from real leaders in Chapter 5.
3. Hop through the commentary.
4. Read every word from beginning to end.
5. Dip your toe in wherever you fancy, maybe starting at the end with 'My living and working assumptions'.
6. Use the index to find what you need.

SYMBOLS

means Watch Out

means Remember This

means Consider This

means 'Secret Sauce'. These are comments about the flavour of my approach to coaching and facilitation. You too have your 'secret sauce' with your own special flavour. With that 'sauce', you, we and I express ourselves in the world – drawing on the 'Secret Source' deep within us.

Endnotes

Endnotes lead to freely available online resources. Go to the Resources section at the end of the book, where you will find the web address.

FOREWORD

Leadership. One of the great privileges in anyone's life is to be invited to lead – an organization, a club, a team, any group endeavour where people come together sharing a common goal and a set of values, and find that they need someone to inspire, motivate, facilitate and convene, meld them into an effective and well-performing unit.

Leadership is an opportunity to be grasped with both hands, to be enjoyed, to be honoured, and to be cherished as a matter of trust, confidence and respect. On good days, it's fun – on bad days, well, that's what this book is all about.

As well as being a great opportunity, leadership is also a very significant responsibility, one that you may well have to face alone, late at night or in the early hours, when you may not be at your best, when you are coping with personal difficulties at home, or when there are those in the organization who strongly disagree with your approach, and who may well be in a position to thwart you.

And that's why this book, *Good Leaders in Turbulent Times*, is such a valuable contribution to the literature on leadership. Martin Farrell, a highly experienced leader himself, explores leadership from the point of view of those who are facing those lonely moments, when the wild waters are lapping at their feet, or are even up to their shoulders and threatening to sweep them away.

But he goes further. He urges leaders to be not just good leaders, but to be the very best leaders they can be, by drawing on such essential human values as decency, justice, fairness, generosity and forgiveness. As all good leaders navigate our turbulent times, living out these core qualities will become ever more vital.

From his extensive work as a mentor, coach, consultant and facilitator, he brings a viewpoint that is both practical, encouraging, empathetic and compassionate.

I first met Martin Farrell in the early 1990s, when I was leading the task of reinspiring and reorganizing the UK work of the British Red Cross. It was a daunting project, and I was looking for someone to support and help manage some 90-odd independent county branches that had been going their own way for far too long. I was struck immediately by Martin's enthusiasm, his energy, his resilience, his readiness to take on any challenge and wrestle it to the ground (sometimes almost literally!). I never saw him daunted, and I never saw him anything less than fascinated by what makes people and teams tick – and work well together.

His many decades of experience shine through this idiosyncratic, engaging, informative and inspiring book, which invites us to learn from leaders' stories of 'wild waters at work' in order to help us better prepare for, survive and emerge stronger from our own.

SIR NICK YOUNG
FORMER CHIEF EXECUTIVE, MACMILLAN CANCER SUPPORT AND BRITISH RED CROSS
CHAIR, MONTE SAN MARTINO TRUST AND TRUSTEE/ADVISOR TO VARIOUS OTHER CHARITIES
1 MAY 2024

INTRODUCTION

Good leaders

The good leaders in this book are everywhere. You probably are one (if you don't think you are now, perhaps you may aspire to become one soon).

Many good leaders are found in organizations everywhere, of which the primary or a significant subsidiary ambition is to build and sustain a civil society that's decent and just, so we and all creatures on Earth can live together well for the foreseeable future. In this book you will see these organizations referred to interchangeably as civil society organizations, charities, not-for-profits, non-profits, voluntary and community sector, NGOs, voluntary organizations, B Corps[1] and third sector organizations.

The aspiring good leaders in this book may occupy leadership positions large and small, as Chairs, board members, CEOs and team leaders.

Whatever your personal home-base – heritage, gender, ability, race, class, sexual orientation, gender, culture, age, faith or none – and whatever leadership style you most identify with, you can be and become a 'Good Leader' by virtue of your keen awareness of your

---

[1] The B in B Corp stands for 'Benefit for all'. Certified B Corporations are businesses that have been certified to benefit all their stakeholders.

responsibility to life on the planet combined with your intention to actively fulfil that responsibility.[2]

As such, you actively water and draw on and practise the wholesome leadership qualities within you, such as generosity, kindness, empathy, forgiveness, decency, integrity, humility enriched by civility, decisiveness and wisdom. There are lots more.

Endnote!

In order to operate well in turbulent times (which, if not yet, will one day inevitably wash into your life) you speak your truth, are vulnerable and are tough – not an iron muscle-pumping kind of tough, but that inner toughness that comes from practising courage, resilience, wisdom and fortitude every day.

While you nourish the wholesome 'seeds' within you, you're also courageous enough not to water the unwholesome qualities within you such as hatred, anger, craving, revenge and denial, which, with unthinking devotion to an ideology, may nourish bloated heroism and delusions of infallibility.

With this practice, you develop the ability to respond – the response-ability – as the moment calls for. One moment may call for ferocious courage, another moment gentle compassion, and all moments will benefit from a good dose of wisdom. You inspire, and followers will be drawn towards you.[3]

---

[2] Often, leadership styles referred to are transformational, thought, strategic, supportive, situational, servant, laissez-faire, facilitative, democratic, coaching, charismatic, bureaucratic, autocratic.

[3] Dr Joan van den Brink *The 3 Companions: Courage Compassion & Wisdom, the Powerful Keys to Happier Work and a Fulfilled Life* (2021).

Endnote²

A good leader moves beyond ego (me, me, me) to eco (us, us, us) and makes decisions not only for now (one year or less) but for future generations (100 years and more). As such you become one of a groundswell of thousands, millions and more good leaders whose collective power arising is enough to withstand and overcome the domination of the few unaware and precariously powerful leaders at the top.[4]

Whatever your position and sector, try putting yourself in the shoes of the other as you read this book. As a board member you may see through the eyes of a CEO, and as CEO or member of a senior team you may seek to better understand the weight on the shoulders of a Chair or board members.

Turbulent times

Wild waters are always at work in our lives, lurking beneath the surface; wild waters are also often at play in our place of work, even in civil society organizations that should be places of safety. The turbulence all around us floods into our work and personal lives and sooner or later will stir up a wild waters experience that will keep us awake at night and nag at us throughout the day. For some it will be a trauma that overwhelms.

Crisis sounds like pretty bad news, which it is at the time. It freezes us, closes us in order to survive. But a crisis is the point at which profound change can come, opening the door to being an even better

---

[4] Otto Scharmer *The Essentials of Theory U: Core Principles and Actions* (2018).

leader and becoming a powerful remedy for others. If faced, reflected upon, digested and integrated, as this book invites you to do, you can navigate your troubles, and be of service to those who follow. We will all be the better for it.

On the other hand, not facing it, not digesting, and not integrating it, will inevitably add to the store of unresolved pain that sooner or later will show up in your life as ill health and in organizational dysfunction.

Your choice.

I have spent my whole career, now in its sixth decade, working in and for civil society organizations. Now, as befits the age and my age, my intention is to encourage and support those who are still out there 'in the fight' for a better world.

My hope is that, faced with accelerating disruptions of social, economic and environmental breakdown, we each find the courage, compassion and wisdom to navigate through our own 'little' stories in order to positively influence the 'big' story of creating the world we want to see.

As aspiring good leaders, we rise to become the best we can be by delving deep into the wholesome resources we carry. As we do this, my and your micro co-creates *our* macro.

That's why I have written this book.

Over to you.

Navigating wild waters, me, you, us all

The boat turned over and I knew this was The End. My wife would be taken by crocodiles and I would be dragged to a watery death under raging wild waters. Our children, who meanwhile were somewhere down river having the time of their lives, would be orphaned.

This was a family holiday with friends in Eswatini, southern Africa to mark my 50th birthday. Our host had jauntily suggested that we pass our second day having a rafting adventure down the Great Usutu river. Adventure indeed it was. In the early morning briefing we were told we must immediately get back in the boat whenever we fell in the water, because the waiting crocs would take us in a flash. I fancied the two guides were joking, but no, this was true Africa, in all its glory.

My thrilling and dangerous journey on that vivid single day more than two decades ago serves as a fitting analogy for the thrills and spills braved by good leaders somewhere, every single day.

- We stepped into the boats, not having done anything remotely like due diligence. Swept along by the thrill of the moment we had little idea of what we were getting into. Leaders who fail to cast a glance at the way ahead may have a thrilling ride but are increasing their chances of falling in wild waters and dragging others in with them.
- Help is at hand. Fortunately, our family of four (a mix of being too old to be able to save ourselves and too young to be bothered) was not alone. Two guides in canoes who had travelled that way before and knew its wild ways were with us the whole way. They, like those who are there to help good leaders, advised us, frequently hauled us out of the wild waters and gave us hope that we would live to tell the tale.
- During our wild waters experience, at several moments I thought I was going to drown. I will never know how close I was, but I vividly remember the moment when the boat was over, not under me. My safety helmet and ill-fitting buoyancy aid around my neck, I could barely breathe. There are moments when leadership can feel like that.
- It was an overwhelming experience. Although there were some moments of relative calm, I spent that whole day well outside my comfort zone. This happens to us as leaders too. Sometimes we are stretched, and then stretched some more to our breaking point. It gets tough.
- In the middle of the eight-hour adventure, we saw no end in sight. The end did come, although as we were nearly there we were greeted by a massive thunder cloud. It was over, but not quite. But

as with times of leadership crisis, the adventure did eventually end. These moments pass, crises come to an end.

- Our family of four had somewhere between very little and no competence in that environment. A good leader might decide to jump in the deep end and take the chance or, as we could have done if we had thought for a moment, we might have chosen to start out by practising somewhere with no crocodiles.
- Much of the Great Usutu river was calm and all the scenery magnificent. But although there was little to see on the surface, there were dangers beneath, such as rocks and debris to entrap us and hungry animals with big teeth. Even when they are not visible, wild waters in organizations are always at work below us, poised to drag us down at any moment.
- In spite of the moments of blind panic, we had a fantastic time, have retold the story on countless occasions and wouldn't have missed it for the world. Leadership can be like that.

Alongside this treacherous adventure, I think often of the several times in my professional life (particularly in 1998, 2000 and 2010/11 with periodic reverberations since then) when things have fallen apart and I have been dragged down, down, down and gasping for air.

I was sure my reputation as a competent and credible person would be destroyed and I would never work again ('I always knew I was an imposter and now the truth is out'). All my friends and acquaintances were seeing me at my most vulnerable, sinking to the muddy bottom of the river.

The pain was overwhelming, and I couldn't bring myself to believe my wife, who repeatedly told me, 'This won't go on forever,' because I was sure that everything was hopeless and endless. A mix of nature, time, meditation, medication, therapy, sharing with 'islands of sanity' communities and the wise counsel of friends, alongside the determination to live, helped me navigate to better days.

These wild water times (which I now see as being related to my earlier life struggles and family heritage) have grown my living and working assumptions (see separate section at end of book) and have become the fuel that nourishes my facilitation and coaching work with civil society leaders. Perhaps it could be the same for you.

I did see the better day that I had thought would never come. Since 2002 (which is also the year of my first international facilitation assignment with the UN) I have been supporting and coaching CEOs in crisis, helping CEOs and board chairs get their professional relationships back on track, and facilitating civil society gatherings of all shapes and sizes in the UK and internationally.

No longer a 'guilty little secret'

While crises scream at us every day in the news, the personal stories of struggle behind them tend to be whispered about behind closed doors. Indeed, those who have signed non-disclosure agreements after leaving a job are explicitly prevented from sharing and learning. As if sharing a guilty little secret, such tales are shared with friends and family in hushed and tearful tones, flavoured with lashings of unexpressed hurt and anger, peppered with shame and awash with feelings of failure and regret.

Alongside all this is a sense that somehow those of us who are working for good should be above all this. Driven by high ideals of decency, justice and playing our part in building a better world, should we not be blessed with a super-abundance of wisdom, grace and patience that overcomes all and renders us immune from overactive ego and greed? Apparently not.

Any one of us can fall into a mess if we allow our unconscious seeds of anger, hatred, denial, othering and the like to rise in us. We are all just a stone's throw from unleashing the wild waters at work within us.

Suffering happens and wild water crises occur in the workplace; they are an inevitable part of life. They have root causes, which can be understood. And it's possible to find our way through, learn and emerge the better for it. There is hope.

Endnote³

So, alongside our aspiration to see a more decent, sustainable world, let's find the courage to try to understand our own struggles and to practise as leaders with as much wisdom as we can muster.

We each start with caring for me, then caring for the other, and then the whole. To start with myself I need to be open to receiving help when I'm so overwhelmed that I can't face it alone. One source of that help is right here – read on.

Fish for invitations, go to the party

A coaching session or a conversation to prepare to facilitate a gathering happens at one time and one place in the flow of the individual's or group's process. This book, however, is for many: you are reading it in your own unique time and place, here, now.

By my writing this book and your reading it, you and I are working together, as we might be in a one-to-one conversation. I have worked to be the best author I can be to serve you in your effort to navigate your wild waters time as best you can.

This is not a step-by-step leader or governance guide or an instruction manual about repairing a tap (do this, do that, fix it). It's a book full of invitations for you to consider and choose if you so wish.

Maybe a metaphor will help? Imagine you are on a fishing trip. Invitations are the fish you want to pull out of the water and hold alive and safe in a net as you consider your next action.

Invitations are lurking on every page – in the story as it unfolds over seven years, in the commentary alongside it, and in Chapter 5 'Passing it on'. Through the lens of your current time and place, please seek out those invitations that seem most pertinent for you, here, now, today. Each invitation is a valuable trigger for you, large and small, which might jump out at you, inspire you, touch you or provoke, while others will pass by unnoticed.

Each invitation you catch is your prompt to stop, to pause and start a process of reflection. Within that space here and now, you may look back to think about what brought you here and look ahead to sense what your future may be.

Some actions will bring immediate benefit. Others need practice and, with focus and concentration, can change our thinking, and changing our thinking can lead to new behaviour. Our new behaviour brings new experiences into our lives, which bring fresh emotions that can generate fresh thinking, which... And so, our lives evolve.

As that happens, we have managed to change our habits, and the physical make-up of our malleable brains has changed too because 'nerve cells that fire together wire together'. Change is possible.[5]

Catching the invitation is just a first step of two, because if you just hold the invite in your hand and don't 'go to the party', nothing will change.

As if this were an invitation to a party, your next step is to decide whether or not you want to accept. If you choose to go the party you are choosing to think and then to plan and proceed by doing something. You will be choosing to thoughtfully respond, not to unthinkingly react.

Make it 'SNAPPY', as explained in Chapter 1, and you too may be saying, 'I'm coming out a better person. I can see beyond the end of my nose,' as a coaching client said to me a year after the worst of the

---

[5] 'Hebbs Rule' developed in 1949 by Donald Hebb, often considered to be the 'father of neuropsychology'.

trauma had passed and they were heading towards integrating their experience.

Your crisis can be a pivot point in your life; mine were for me. I wish you the courage, compassion and wisdom you will need to find your new way.

PROLOGUE (SEVEN YEARS)

That Chapter 1 plays on a Tuesday, one year and a day before the characters hit their 'wild Wednesdays' experiences, and in Chapters 3 and 4 are portrayed as being on a Thursday and Friday, is a convenient fiction. The revealing of the story over these weekdays symbolizes a truth: neither the nine characters nor any of us are alone. While we are going through our stuff, so are many others on that same day somewhere, albeit unbeknown to us.

While we struggle feeling alone on our 'wild Wednesday', so are many others whom we will never know. While we are noticing (or failing to notice) red flags warning of trouble ahead, there will be other leaders elsewhere doing the same. While we are digesting a year later and integrating our experiences five years later, there will be others digesting and integrating as we are.

That Chapter 5 is a Monday is also a convenient fiction with a tucked away truth within it. These Monday contributions are from real-life leaders (CEOs) who, having done the inner work to digest and integrate their wild waters experiences, are able to become a remedy for others. The beginning of a new week symbolizes that they are well down the track of integrating their experiences and are setting off anew. May their learning inform us.

While every civil society leader I have supported and every board and every gathering I have facilitated is unique, there are common themes. I convey some of these through the characters, who are entirely fictional.

Some of the fictional characters' stories may ring true for you, from your own or others' wild waters experiences. Some may ring *so* true that you think I have written about you. Well, I haven't – if I happen to know your story, it is and will always be held in strict confidence.

In the first four chapters, we follow fictional characters on a trip through everyday events, infused with their private fears, fantasies and inner dialogue. Things don't make sense anymore as worlds are turned upside down and seemingly crazy stuff is happening.

Here are the fictional characters in order of appearance

Robin, 45, is CEO of a hospice and is worried about a big capital project being pushed robustly by a small group of board members.

Tara, 42, is CEO of a heritage sector charity and is trying hard to get on with her new Chair, who has a very different style from his much-appreciated predecessor.

Grace, 57, CEO of a community homelessness organization, is facing up to the fact that her Chair is soon to leave after 26 years.

Sarah, 38, is founder Chair of a disability organization and has just appointed the third CEO in as many years.

Bob, 32, a first-time CEO with a history of petty crime, is excited to be taking over from the long-serving first director of a youth organization.

Daniel, 58, approaching retirement, a long-standing Chair, has just managed to persuade his board members to appoint Bob.

Rose, 52, is a CEO facing the prospect of a merger and being out of the job that she has been doing for decades.

Alice, 28, has just been appointed CEO of Sarah's charity and can't fathom the budget, which just doesn't add up.

Imran, 31, on impulse stops to buy a magazine from a street seller and a year later realizes this was a turning point in his life.

CHAPTER 1
SOMETHING'S BREWING

STAY AWAKE, NOTICE

A year and a day before wild Wednesday, we meet the characters at a conference. Some are troubled. A few notice a threatening smell of smoke, as alarm bells ring for everyone...

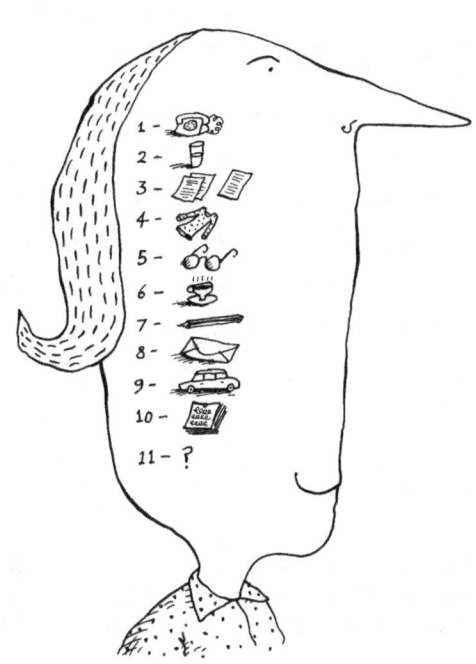

Robin (is glued to his laptop)

It was a conference like any other. Or so it seemed. The quiet clatter of crockery and the easy chit-chat hum of the servers in their neat uniforms would soon be drowned out by a flood spilling out from the morning breakout sessions.

But not quite yet. For a few minutes longer a reassuringly expectant calm hung in the air this Tuesday morning, held by the uplifting words of the opening keynote and occasional laughter and applause spilling from breakout rooms.

Dotted around the room were a few lone hunched figures. Heads down, tucked away in corners, each a safe distance away from the multi-coloured stands and eager exhibitors.

None of the figures looked up, but were glued to their laptops, tablets and phones, gazing intently at their screens as if their lives depended on it. Maybe it did. So many emails pouring into the inbox. What they saw there had been more pressing than the wisdoms being dispensed in the morning sessions. None were tempted by the variety of rich offerings.

Disruption and overload is a feature of our times. That's how it is and will be, as far as we can see. When I was at the British Red Cross in the 1990s there was constant talk of 'managing change'; now the conversation is about the need for adaptation and resilience in the face of permanent volatility, perpetual uncertainty, complexity and ambiguity that penetrate every professional relationship, every board meeting and every email.

Good leaders minimize the impact on them from outside by minimizing disruption on the inside.

This was an annual gathering of civil society leaders and those who aspired to be so, who had turned up in their hundreds to network, learn some new stuff and return to the ranch with renewed vigour.

Tucked away in a comfy corner armchair, the smell of the coffee reached Robin, who actually wanted to be sitting in a forest. But unfortunately, forests were not on offer at this conference. The demands of his screen were even more compelling than the siren temptations of coffee, chocolate muffins and the imagined fragrance of nature.

'I'll just check a few more mails, and anyway I've been overdoing the caffeine recently,' he reasoned, remembering what his wife, who was far away facing a class of primary school children, was always telling him. 'You should cut down on sugar too, and chew everything 32 times,' she advised. Wise words, ignored.

All that we consume creates us. Beyond food and drink, the films we choose to see, books we read, TV we watch, conversations we have and all we take in, feed the potential within us, for good or ill. Protecting ourselves is especially vital when we are stressed and vulnerable. *Endnote*

The next thing Robin knew, he was heading back to his laptop with a cappuccino and almond croissants (one of his several guilty little secrets).

You know your unhealthy habits well; your cosy bedfellows, you live with them every day. You want to part company, but you don't. Feeding your unhealthy habit will not end well.

If you are tired of your habits, consider this. Stop, stand in front of a mirror and look yourself in the eye. Name your habit, say or write what's good about it and what's not. Then choose. If you decide to interrupt your habit, say it out loud, write it, tell a friend.

There had been talk recently about launching a big capital project at his hospice and he had to be sure he wasn't going to miss anything. Not only that, but his appraisal was coming up soon, the first for some years.

Robin really wasn't at all sure that a big capital project was such a good idea, but a couple of the trustees (successful builders who said they knew about this sort of thing) were very energized about it and were angling to get the whole board onside. They were pressing the Chair for a thorough appraisal of the CEO, saying it was about time. The recently retired and soon-to-stand-down Chair had questioned it, 'Everything okay, is it?' before giving in.

Head buried in his emails, Robin didn't notice the muffled applause from one of the breakout rooms. He wasn't listening. He was too busy trying to keep his head above water. Robin was troubled and longed not to be deep in thought, but deep in nature.

Far from the ancient woodlands of his fantasy, the room was now beginning to buzz with outpourings from the workshops. *Time for more coffee*, thought Robin. The glow of his laptop screen faded as he gathered up his stuff.

Heading for the queue, not for the first time, he imagined he felt a tap on the shoulder that was more like a sharp finger poke. It brought to mind a saying he had once heard somewhere: 'What do you already know that you're going to find out in a year?'

Fearing he was being followed by some malcontent, Robin turned around. He saw no one but was sorely troubled when he caught a glimpse of himself in an old mirror.

For the rest of his day, that same little phrase, 'What do you already know…' kept on rolling around like an echoing thunderclap.

'What do you already know that you're going to find out in a year?' tells us that the signs are there but we are not noticing them. As time goes on, the message gets louder but still you don't notice. In a year, or thereabouts, the signs get so loud you can't miss them. It's better to listen now to that weak signal than it is to wait until the mess hits the fan.[6]

Unsteady on his feet, Robin felt a shiver as he stood up. *Got to look after myself,* he reasoned, *can't get sick, there's too much going on at work.*

Seeing his reflection, now he started worrying about attire. Smart casual, the conference instructions had said. *Am I overdressed? Do I look okay?*

Too many worries. *Now I'm going to have to see a psychotherapist, as well as a physio for my shoulder. Must make that appointment.*

Heading towards the coffee queue, the crowd's buzzing got louder as his inner chatter went along with him: *... in a year... smart enough... therapist...* The outer hubbub soon drowned out his inner babble.

Tara (scribble, scribble, scribble)

Perilously close to inducements free for the taking, Tara was scribbling, furiously. In a couple of weeks she would have a first formal meeting with her new Chair, whose appointment had just

---

[6] Credited to Amy Christianson and quoted in Nancy Kline *Time to Think: Listening to Ignite the Human Mind* (1999) p83.

been approved after a lengthy external recruitment process. After many years as a big shot in business, he proclaimed it was time to 'give something back'.

On his very first day he had mailed a mountain of stuff to read, asked her for a report of all current activities and the planning assumptions for next year's draft budget. Although somewhat taken aback by the bluntness of his demands, Tara, keen to show her best side, put it down to beginner's enthusiasm. *Yes*, she thought, *he's keen, hitting the ground running, that's okay.*

An idealist with a lifelong interest in heritage and ancestry, Tara was inclined to take the long view and see the better side of people. Inspired by the generous world view of her Irish and Indian parents, she was on a mission to make today's world a better place. Always super-diligent, she put in more hours than was good for her. She knew that, but couldn't stop.

CAUGHT IN AN UNDERCURRENT

But right now she couldn't get the words right, so was trying to get her thoughts straight by doing a brain dump: scribble, scribble, scribble. Everything was tangled inside her dizzy head, and she hoped the tangle would straighten itself out if she let it pour out in an unfettered stream of consciousness.

'Get it out of your head and onto paper,' a wise woman once said. Letting the words pour out onto paper is a quick, cheap and effective way of clearing your mind when you are in a muddle.

Start where you are: 'I don't know what to write... this is so annoying... why the hell don't those people understand...' and go from there.

Occasionally, Tara still met up socially with the previous Chair, who had come to the end of his third term and had stood down with fanfare and bouquets. She often found herself thinking about him. He had been liked and appreciated by everyone in the head office and the regions and was already sadly missed, especially by Tara, who had found him easy to work with. The ease about him reminded her of her Irish dad.

Not only that, but he had been quite a smooth operator in social situations, especially the grand ones. A celebrity had come to speak at the organization's centenary celebration and the Chair had worked his magic. They were so impressed with the work of the heritage sector that they immediately accepted the Chair's invitation to do the keynote at the next conference. The Chair had been good at that kind of thing – friendly and canny too.

Unlike his successor, he hadn't insisted on being called 'Chair*man*'. Although mostly hands-off, he had always been to hand when needed, just a phone call away.

The for-now easy chatter of the first few arriving in the coffee queue didn't distract Tara as her pen scribbled. But after a while, as the noise swelled, her hand slowed. Enough for now.

As she joined the stream of conversations spilling from group sessions, she feared she had missed out on some gems.

She recalled that she had an uneasy feeling when she and her new Chair had met during the recruitment process, he with his clipped tone and distant demeanour. She couldn't say why, but it just didn't feel right. Being the owner of a successful company, he had impressed the recruitment committee with his show of financial acumen. Money mattered, they had reasoned, especially at this time of instability.

Before coming to their decision, trustees asked her opinion, but she couldn't quite find the words to describe her reservations, so she acquiesced to their view that he was probably the best of the bunch. She had noticed her back stiffening the very first time they met; he was not her first choice.

Listen to first impressions. Maybe you don't yet know what they mean but your first impression contains a truth. Speak up, speak up, don't allow your truth to be brushed aside. If you only have a hazy notion of your truth, ask for time to think, sleep on it, speak with someone who is good at listening without interruption.

Soon after he was formally installed as Chair, Tara often found herself on the receiving end of his PA's polite but firm request to meet him at his offices at 8am. Tara's back went tight every time she heard that clipped voice. This was certainly not her preferred time of day, but she didn't want to ruffle feathers, so she just said, 'Okay, that's fine.'

Some months later she found herself regretting her meek acquiescence and criticized herself for not having spoken her mind. She resolved to reframe the 'what ifs' that plagued her with 'what was', accepting and even embracing what had happened, and moving on.

It's obvious but true: newness shakes things up. A new Chair or trustee, a new CEO or senior team members shake things up. That shaking can work for good or ill, so be especially attentive when new things happen.

Robin and Tara (have landed in the same place)

Meanwhile, with her scribbles still in hand, Tara headed for the drinks queue. Eager for their caffeine or healthy option fix, chattering delegates from breakout sessions were smelling the coffee and herbal infusions and were forming a not-so-orderly queue.

In the converging crowd, by some happy chance, Robin and Tara, for one more moment still strangers to each other, landed at the same spot. 'After you,' smiled Robin, kindly. 'Looks like you've been working hard,' he observed, seeing Tara's scribbly notepad.

'Well yes, sort of working hard, but I'm not getting anywhere.' As they edged towards the neatly laid out cups and bubbling urn, she was not able to restrain herself and told the story of her Chair (*man*) and how she felt she had to choose her words so very carefully.

'Problem is, I don't know which words to choose nor what order to put them in. That's all.' She smiled weakly.

Good leaders are not satisfied with being passive two-dimensional observers, as if watching a nature documentary on TV. They remain curious about how they got those amazing images, what's going on behind the scenes, how it came to be that way and what may come to pass.

What was that tension in the air at the board meeting... why do we always get stuck when... what's going on between this and that person... how are people's personal lives (ageing parents, growing children, illnesses, personal dramas and the rest) impacting their working day?

Effective leaders seek to understand what's on the inside, not only what's reached the surface.

An experienced and diligent third sector manager of some decades, writing had always come easily to Tara. But writing this note was anything but. She couldn't get her frozen hand to move the right way, felt incompetent and ached for it to be otherwise.

Just then, her eye chanced upon the little warming flame under the urn, and the glimpse of it warmed her. She knew it was just a little flame, but she fancied it was smiling to unfreeze her hand.

Now at the head of the queue, the server's routine interrupted her daydreaming. 'Tea, coffee? Milk, sugar, over there.'

Drink in hand, Tara felt some relief – she loved her lattes – or maybe because of the unexpected moment of sharing with a stranger. *Hmm, it's good to talk*, she thought. *These conferences are good for that. The breaks are the best bit. A good chat and a bit of fellow feeling does you good.*

Seeing Robin's bundled papers, she said, 'What are you up to?'

'I've been trying to be healthier but, well you know, I'll start tomorrow', Robin said with a weak smile.

Living in your past, or indeed in your future, is not as rich as living in the present. Consider the possibility of leading your life by 'letting go and letting come' and being led by the 'emerging future'. Letting go of what no longer serves us and looking in the direction of what's emerging will help us live well. It may also help us to die wise when our time comes. *Endnote*[5]

And so it was that with fresh brews in hand and each content to have chanced upon some fellow feeling, Robin and Tara headed for a couple of comfy chairs over in the corner, away from the crowd, but barely a few steps away from the old mirror that Robin had thought was speaking to him just a few moments before.

Grace (is listening)

A woman appeared, well dressed, with a sober briefcase that had seen a lot of life. Cautiously balancing a cup of camomile, she was heading towards that same quiet-ish corner a few steps away from that old mirror.

Being a civil society event, there was a spirit of generosity in the air. Seeing Grace, rather than grabbing two chairs for himself and Tara Robin kindly offered, 'Will you join us, shall I get another chair?'

Having arrived late the previous night after a long train journey, and after an unsettled night in a cheap hotel on a noisy road, she was glad of Robin's natural kindness.[7] With an audible sigh of relief – her back was still troubling her – she lowered herself into a comfy chair oasis to enjoy her tea.

'Get another chair? Good idea,' said Tara with a conspiratorial smile. 'That's what we're talking about. New Chairs. I've just got a new one and he's told me to sort out next year's budget. I've done a first draft of the numbers okay, but now I'm stuck with the cover note. Don't know why. Just can't get my head around it. He said he must have everything on his desk tomorrow morning. I had a lovely relationship with the old Chair, but this new one...'

---

[7] See Graham Allcott *Kind: The Quiet Power of Kindness at Work* (2024).

The chairs were comfy, and the drinks were warm. Robin told his story of the enthusiastic trustees pushing for the capital project and Tara told her story of the new Chair recruited because he knew about money.

Grace was listening with curiosity and genuine interest, pausing her own inner chatter about her Chair, who had just announced his retirement after 26 years. She had noticed that he wasn't there like he used to be and was becoming ever more absent-minded. A vacuum.

Grace noticed a woman with pink hair chatting with an enthusiastic young guy offering a QR code with contact details. But Grace was no longer one for working the room. Been there, done that. A kind and gracious soul, she was a conference veteran and had long since learned it was smart to rest from the melee whenever possible.

'What's all that about then?' Grace asked herself. 'How come such a simple thing is so hard?' Her experiences of working with young people in her church inner-city project in her early 20s had taught her to be kind and compassionate, and resilient with it. Now called to be an executive director of a project serving the homeless and destitute in a northern city, she knew about the rough end of life. And she also knew how to listen, with full attention.

'Silent' is an anagram of 'listen' – being silent helps us listen.

Tara found herself taken aback by this unexpected kindness of a stranger. Being on the receiving end of this direct question touched some long-buried place inside her and she was touched by a shiver. *Yes indeed, why is this so hard?* She knew, but until this very moment had all but forgotten. But now she was dragged back by memories she had left behind.

Robin and Grace were taken back a decade to the time when things had gone so very wrong in Tara's previous job. Feelings in the manor house and museum of which Tara had been CEO were running high with erudite arguments about the relative merits of conservation and restoration; things had got well out of hand.

A polarising debate had ensued between preserving the old and hunger for the new, with some favouring maintenance of rural tranquillity and others pushing commercial interests and the need for expansion. 'We have to keep up with the times,' they had said. Volunteers in the house and garden got involved and then the trustees piled in too. All together they created a right old mess.

Seemingly for hours as the minutes passed, Tara touched memories that had been held unmoving, as if set in amber. The power of deep listening had created enough safety in this noisy room for her to be reminded of her long-buried struggles.

With practice, listening can become our superpower. If we stop talking, allow space for the other, connect with what happens inside us as we listen, we can expand our innate capacity to listen beyond our ears. Of the four levels of listening, the fourth, 'generative listening', is the one in which the 'highest future possibility' becomes visible. Open to discovery, the listened to and the listener are both changed. *Endnote*[6]

Tears came up too, but now was not the time let them go, although they did find their way to the surface some days later.

Robin and Grace's listening helped Tara dive back into her old story about how she had tried and tried – and cried – until she finally decided she had done enough. The time had come to paddle to calmer waters, so she resigned.

A choice to be a leader in civil society is also a choice to face and overcome challenges. Struggles go with the territory. That's how it is.

But if you find your work is taking an unacceptable toll on you and has become too punishing, think again – have you done enough, at least for now? It's okay to move on.

Tara hadn't looked back.

Until now.

Quite quickly she had landed her new position running a heritage charity job, with multiple sites and more influence to bring about positive change. She had immediately hit it off with her new Chair and the whole board. Couldn't be better. Until the Chair left, and a new one arrived.

The announcement for the second morning sessions interrupted her recollections and the conference babble flooded their corner sanctuary. 'What did you think of the opening keynote?' 'What session are you going to?' 'Yes, we had one of those too …' 'What do you think of it so far?'

She blinked and looked at Robin and Grace, grateful for how readily their kind attention and listening had flicked an inner release key. Looking at her scribbles, she thought, *I'll have another go at that later.*

As they drifted in the general direction of the breakout rooms, Tara noticed a plate with a single leftover croissant, and for an instant was nudged by a familiar deep-down lonely feeling. But as she threw a smile back to Robin and Grace, she was grateful for their generous listening and fellow feeling and knew she wasn't alone after all.

Remember that you are surrounded by fellow travellers, a host of good leaders all creating a better future. Take the initiative, contact another leader and collaborate. Fellow feeling is awaiting your call.

Good morning, my name is Sarah (I'm a founder)

Sarah was feeling out of place. Although she had founded her charity some five years earlier, this was the first civil society conference she had ever been too. She had been thinking for a while that she really should be better acquainted with how other charities do things. And anyway, coming down to London gave her the chance to stay over with her nephew, now in his final year of law studies, following family tradition.

If this is the first time you have been involved in a third sector organization, especially if you are in a position of influence, connect with other civil society leaders in your professional or geographical area and encourage each other. Don't delay.

Sarah launched uneasily into the fray of the morning break, thinking of her friends with whom she regularly met for tea and chat. *I can tell them all about it next week*, she thought.

Wondering if she might be somewhat overdressed and stand out too much, Sarah carried her conference bag in front of her like a buffer between her and this unfamiliar world.

The fully recyclable cloth bags and conference pens carrying a clarion call to 'Believe in Better' had both been designed by children with learning disabilities. *If they do the same next year*, Sarah thought, *I'll get all our names on it. Why not? That would get our name out there.*

Never one to miss an opportunity, she made a mental note to call her designer friend to see if she could come up with some ideas. Sarah had contacts and could move and shake.

You have just come up with a cracking good idea; what's your next action? If you're a Chair or trustee and your new idea is a short-term operational matter, your next action should be to pass it on to your CEO. If you are the CEO and this has broader long-term implications, your next action is to put it on the list for your next conversation with your Chair or responsible board member. Doing otherwise will most likely end in tears.

Huddles of chattering delegates were now drifting to workshops in the quaintly named breakout rooms. On her way to her session for charity founders, appropriately taking place in a room named 'Passion', Sarah saw a sign to the 'Shine a Light On Workplace Bullying' session, which conference organizers had cleverly placed in a room called 'Transparency' but which, somewhat less cleverly, was tucked away at the end of a long, dark corridor.

Bullying is abhorrent anywhere and must not be tolerated in civil society organizations. As a leader, do not allow bullying behaviour. Don't do it, stop it if you see it, stand up to it if it is happening to you. As soon as you get a sniff of it, take action. Of course.

If you are a victim, get help. Now. When you are bullied by someone in power over you, you start to doubt your own judgement and your own worth. 'Coercive control' is when another person asserts his or her world view onto you as being one in which he or she is always right and you are always wrong. Get help to rediscover what's true.

Thinking that she should be looking out for Alice, her recently appointed CEO, Sarah hurried to her chosen session, 'Founder Flounder'. As she entered the room named 'Passion', she scanned faces, some of which returned her uncertain smile, while others studied the list of participants.

There was a slightly furtive mood in the room. Uncharacteristically, she found herself unsure about what she would say about herself if there was a round of introductions.

Founders sometimes get a bad rap. A prejudice hangs in the air that they might be over-engaged and unable to let go of their baby when the time comes. That can happen, but let's remember how many of the UK's 200,000 or so charities would exist, including the big ones, if it hadn't been for that founding passion to propel an idea from the kitchen table into the world. Let's celebrate their contribution.

Tucking herself away at the back of the room, Sarah was relieved that there were to be no awkward introductions. After a swift opening word from the session facilitator, the presenter opened her first slide. Sarah noticed that there was '1 of 27' at the bottom of the screen, each with colourful images garnished with a few well-chosen words. Doubting that there really was so much to be said about being a founder, she wondered whether she was wasting her time and found herself thinking she might leave part-way through and pop into another session – maybe the one next door with the sporadic bursts of laughter. (The grass is always greener...)

But she was pleasantly surprised. Still listening when slide '7 of 27' landed on the screen, Sarah found herself smiling at the spirited young woman who just five years earlier as a 21-year-old student had set up an environmental charity collaborating with student volunteers in South America. *Hmm*, she pondered, *founders come in all ages, shapes and sizes.*

Speaking touchingly about her own experience, the presenter explained how she had struggled when the board members, each of whom she had appointed, decided it was time for her to move aside and to appoint the organization's first full-time director. She had allowed herself to be persuaded and faced the daunting prospect of passing her 'cherished baby' into the arms of a stranger. She knew it was time for her and for her baby to grow up.

Although she had certainly struggled to let go and remained passionate about her baby, she had founded other ventures through which to express her apparently boundless zeal. *All rather impressive*, thought Sarah. *My word, what these young people get up to!*

As the presenter shared her youthful wisdoms, Sarah's mind drifted off to the time when her very own very real flesh-and-blood baby was diagnosed with a disorder and didn't make it to his first birthday. That was a distant six years ago and the memory was fading painfully slowly, and she had found some solace in setting up her own charity.

Through her county network she had pulled together a group of concerned parents who had channelled their distress and energies into setting up the charity. Fired with enthusiasm around their kitchen tables, they had set about getting things off the ground, with Sarah leading the charge.

There had been no relevant provision at all in the county and, with the support of some contacts, Sarah's husband eased a funding application on its way. Soon there was interest from neighbouring counties and things took off when grants for training appeared.

Prompted by the spirited young presenter, Sarah remembered how she and her friends had been run off their feet and after a couple of years decided to step up a gear and appoint their first director. A big step, not easily taken.

The early days had been a terribly upsetting time and it wasn't that good now either with a bouncy new CEO taking up her post and wanting to change everything. It hadn't worked out well with the two previous directors, each of whom departed through a revolving door just a matter of months after arriving.

She winced as she remembered allowing herself to be persuaded by two new trustees who had argued forcibly for the bright young Alice ('Give her a chance,' they had said) in preference to the candidate she had seen as safer and indeed more biddable.

Even though she did not greatly relish the prospect of meeting her, she resolved to try to find Alice, maybe in the lunch break. *If it doesn't work out today, we can always catch up at the next board meeting, can't we?* she reasoned.

If you have a hunch that a conversation needs to happen, especially if you are troubled by the thought of it, don't delay, do it today. Yes it's hard and, yes, be courageous.

Sarah was jolted out of her daydream by the workshop presenter saying, 'And last but by no means least...' She spoke with a wisdom beyond her years about the benefits of a proper induction and the importance of the Chairs and CEOs working together to create and sustain the 'fine balance' needed for things to flourish.

Maybe, thought Sarah, she should have been more involved when Alice started and not have left her induction to the staff team. With that and wanting to get full value for her conference fee, which she had paid out of her own pocket, she slipped out, hopefully unheard and unseen, to try another session.

Surveying the empty corridors with humming conversations behind closed doors, she chanced upon a sign announcing a 'Don't Drift into Crisis' session. She sneaked into the session and tried unsuccessfully to hide by the door.

She was just in time to see a slide advising: 'Chairs and CEOs – build trust from day one'. She winced. Guilty as charged.

She wanted again to slip out unnoticed, but the presenter's welcoming smile, swiftly cast in her direction, kept her rooted to the spot. It would be impolite now that she had been noticed; little did she know that she would soon be told to leave.

Bob (rebelling mostly illegally) bumps into Rose (rebelling mostly legally)

In the room right next to the coffee area, Bob led the loud applause as the morning breakout session closed. From his front-row spot, he had enjoyed every minute of it. *Right up my street*, he thought, *this media stuff, love it*. He was finding that he was a natural in front of a mic, and now three months in post he reckoned it was high time to find out how the professionals do it.

Excited to be in his first CEO role at such a tender young age, he had signed up for the conference in his very first week. The 'Media for Youth Work' session had jumped off the webpage and he had ticked the box without hesitation.

Born into an inner-city estate, he had drifted into all sorts of trouble and at 14 was up in court facing a custodial sentence. His mum was tearful and furious in equal measure and blamed herself. 'My little Bobby, what have I done wrong?' Little Bobby's dad was long gone and not available for comment.

Leaving his baby name behind, Bob (more street cred) remembers being interviewed by a youth worker who was inspiring and told him he might avoid being locked up if he agreed to come to a community youth project that had been set up as an alternative to custody.

Sure, he agreed, seeing it as a soft option. The Junction Project, they called it – you know, it's your life, it's time for you to choose to go this way or that.

To cut a rocky short story even shorter, he discovered it wasn't quite as soft as he had imagined. Those youth workers just kept on trying to get him to think for himself, not just to follow the older kids from the estate. He dodged the law well enough and in time earned his place as leader of a notorious gang of younger kids who in turn found it all too easy to follow the crowd. Now he was the big guy with arms full of tattoos and homemade 'Love' and 'Hate' on his knuckles. He neither thought about tomorrow nor, as the social workers kept insisting, did he 'consider the consequences of his actions'.

The youth workers did their very best to help him. A one-time bank robber who had paid for his misdemeanours behind bars had been hired by the project to hard-talk the kids about the reality of a life of crime.

Delivered with a punch of raw truth, the message landed and one day something clicked: *Knocking off other peoples' stuff and ducking and diving is a mug's game,* he reasoned and *I need more steady cash and a lot less hassle.*

A couple of lucky breaks later Bob had a regular job as builder and plasterer, earning good money. He remembers rolling up at the Junction parking his shiny second-hand van on a double yellow and swaggering in to offer the kids a couple of weeks' work experience. Bob the builder they had called him, and the name stuck.

'You've got to help out those kids,' he told the staff. 'They're going through shit.' How knowing, how very wise.

Back in the day it was easier. 'Kids these days have it harder,' he said. So now, with a bit of life on the clock and some cash in the bank, he thought he would do his bit.

He had been doing sessional youth work for a couple of years. Not only that, but he'd had enough of plastering (see one wall and you have seen the lot) and was confident he could step up in the world.

A mate told him about a well-established youth project in a neighbouring borough. The founding director had decided it was time to move on and the trustees thought it was time for the project to open a new chapter, especially with its quarter-century celebration coming up. There were dissenting voices on the board, but in the end, despite his limited experience, Daniel, the very wise Chair, and some trustees saw Bob's potential, took a risk and made the offer.

With a couple of others on the board, it was Daniel the Chair, with a wisdom born of decades of experience in race relations and who worked in government, who finally swung the decision. He knew Bob had a compelling story to tell and would hit the ground running. And so it was that Bob landed his dream job.

Aware that the Fairtrade coffee (not his regular tipple but he thought he would give it a try) and cake was next on the agenda, and heading for the door, Bob found himself next to that woman who had been asking a lot of questions. Some decades his senior, he had been aware of her throughout the workshop, with her arty clothes and pink hair.

'She was good, wasn't she,' he said, nodding in the direction of the workshop presenter, a senior manager at a charity communications agency. 'She knew her stuff, she'll go far.'

'Well, yes, sure she had some good new ideas but most of it I've heard before,' said Rose with the pink hair. 'I've seen things come and go and then come round again and get served up in new ways. Like pasta, it's all basically the same but comes in different shapes, sizes and colours. But some things change. This communications business is different from when I started out in community arts. We were on a mission to fight the establishment and we made a lot of noise. Quite colourful too.' She smiled.

In spite of, maybe because of, their difference in age, gender and background, they immediately hit it off. They had more in common than divided.

That 'we have more in common than divides us' is easy to say but it's hard to put into practice. Have a go at living it, minute by minute, every thought, word, action, just for one day. Today, now. It's so worth it.

'I tell you what though,' she said to Bob, 'she was on the button when she said that if you have too many people wanting to jump in front of the camera you can get into a bit of a bun fight. Messes things up.'

Her words were drowned out by the noise of the crowd. Bob heard, but he wasn't listening.

How strong is your drive to be noticed, to be recognized as successful and famous? Ego is one of the drivers that gets us out of bed to do stuff, but you will be heading down a rocky road if you allow your ego to be in the driving seat.

As they inched forward in the queue, Bob discovered that this was Rose, who had founded a community arts project nearly four decades ago, straight from art college. He was intrigued to hear about her youthful rebellion conducted mainly legally, while noting that he and his mates had rebelled mainly illegally. *Funny old world*, he thought.

She told him about how a group of art students, fired up with the audacity of youth and a passion for what creative expression could bring the world, had set up an evening art project for the local community. 'Those were the days, my friend, we thought they'd never end.' Rose spoke of the powder keg of struggle and hope during those years of right-leaning government and how a few years later they were showered with funding and accolades from the new left-leaning government. No longer one of the *enfants terribles*, they found themselves being celebrated as the 'cutting edge' of change, for which she won awards and prizes.

Bob (is smelling smoke)

Thinking that it would set the right tone for the conference, the organizers had chosen aspirational names for conference breakout rooms. Guests were variously told that their meetings would be in 'Hope', 'Life', 'Truth', 'Trust', 'Passion' and such like.

Although they had each signed up for different sessions, Rose and Bob were so engrossed in their refreshment break exchanges that they let themselves be carried by the crowd. The chatty flow landed them in 'Trust', the room chosen for the 'Don't Drift Into Crisis' session.

You can't weigh it, count it or see it. This little word has a 't' at both ends and is one of your most valuable tools in your leadership kitbag: trust… earn it.

Presenters Chris and Tom, who were both lawyers, had a professional style that exuded an air of confidence. They were not surprised to see the level of interest in their talk; they had seen many good leaders drift into crisis. Standing room only with a few hovering around the door, not wanting to be too close to talk of crisis, perhaps fearing they might catch it. Nor were they sure that being seen in such company would further their careers; being seen to admit their struggles felt like revealing a guilty little secret into a cruel world. *What will people think?*

Self-assured Chris began: 'We have advised many CEOs during times of crisis with their employers and vice versa. This workshop is about the most common symptoms that we see that have led to a crisis and the need for legal advice. There are many things you can do to reduce your chances of drifting onto the rocks. It's much better to avoid the rocks than to get stuck and struggle to get off them.'

Have you heard the story? When the ship had run aground in stormy seas, the captain radioed the coastguard for advice. 'Mayday! Mayday! What should I do?' After a short pause, the coastguard's booming voice responded, 'Do not let your ship get into this position.' And then again, even more boomingly, 'I repeat, do not let your ship get into this position.'

Good advice. Do not be the captain of that ship. Getting off the rocks is harder than noticing red flags telling you there's danger ahead.

A list of bullet-point headlines flashed onto the screen. As his eyes landed on '… breakdown of trust…', Bob's nose twitched. He knew this smell. With a quick sniff and a furrowed brow, Bob turned to Rose, his new best friend and said, 'Hey, do you smell smoke? There's something in the air.'

'Hmm maybe,' she said, 'not sure'.

Warming to her subject, Chris began to introduce the issues she suggested civil society leaders should always keep in mind.

'… the most common reason for a board asking a CEO to leave is a breakdown of trust between trustees or with the senior management team…

… do not allow a deficit of trust and hope to accumulate…

… apportioning blame is less effective than taking action…

… be courageous and communicate, especially with those people with whom you find it most difficult…

… instead of facing up to the real issue of trust, boards often try to find performance or conduct fault and then make flimsy accusations, which can lead to the suspension of the CEO and the start of disciplinary proceedings…'

Resist the impulse to blame another. Better to look to yourself
and do what you need to do to make something better.

'Actually, I think I do smell something funny,' whispered Rose.
Scanning the crowded room, she caught the eye of only one other
who, with a bemused sniffing of the air and furrowed brow, returned
Rose's questioning expression. No one else seemed bothered; all were
looking at Chris, whose wisdoms continued to pour forth unabated.

'…CEOs' positions are very rarely made redundant, as an organization
usually needs a leader (although some CEOs may be offered reduced
time or reduced pay and benefits)…

…if things do begin to go wrong, then the position can very quickly
take a turn for the worse, so don't leave it and just hope it'll get
sorted by itself. Wake up to what's happening around you and take
action to build and retain the trust of the board, senior team and…'

Consciously act in ways that will build and sustain trust – it's
the oxygen that nourishes healthy and productive relationships.
With trust, those who follow your lead can lower their guard and
are more able to give of their best. Those who follow willingly
give leaders their effort and simply ask in return that their
leaders stay true and earn that trust each day. Trust can easily be
dented or lost in one careless moment, so cherish it. *Endnote*

At that moment, a piercing alarm bell went off somewhere in the building. Shaken but not unduly stirred by the interruption, Chris was about to offer yet more good advice when a young man sporting a tangerine 'Here to Help' T-shirt rushed into the room.

The bell, the 'Here to Help' man and a smell of burning sucked attention away from the screen. Crisis was closer than anyone had realized.

As Chris asked for the 'next slide please' (which fittingly advised 'Wake up to what's happening – take action' and was espousing the virtues of good communication), a tangerine T-shirted 'Here to Help' woman crashed into the room. She and 'Here to Help' man exchanged loud whispers.

As 'Here to Help' woman crashed out to spread the breaking news, 'Here to Help' man announced with barely concealed panic, 'There's a fire, not a practice, have to leave the building, um… *now!*'

As 50 people gathered themselves up to leave with a mix of resignation (probably *is* a false alarm?) and a twist of existential panic, some glanced at headlines of the 'Wake Up' set of slides that, having slipped into slideshow mode, were silently scrolling undeterred by the rising chaos all around. '… collaborate… build trust… avoid blaming… be courageous… face the real issue… wake up…'

Informed by years of helping struggling charities, Chris had more good advice to offer and had put it on handouts to give out later:

1. Chair, trustees and CEO should agree goals, priorities and a clear strategy with reasonable expectations and measurable goals.
2. Make sure all trustees understand their responsibilities, avoid duplication of effort and agree boundaries between the executive and governance roles.

3. Once a year or agreed frequency have an appraisal for the CEO and also have the board appraise its own performance.
4. Undertake governance training for trustees.
5. Agree how, when, in what form communication between trustees and senior team will happen and stick to it.
6. Make sure there are no 'surprises', both about strategic and operational matters, especially when things are not going to plan.

Alice (is arriving late)

As she surfaced from an awkward slumber on the much delayed 06.22 from the north, Alice tried to disentangle what she saw flashing past the window from the lingering scraps of her dreams. Her daydreams were feeling very real.

She had been awake half the night with their two-year-old and figured she may as well have taken an even earlier train. With this one, hit by the delays, she was going to miss most of the morning; most embarrassing and not good at all, as her Chair, Sarah, might be looking for her.

The images of passing north London suburbs were blurringly overlaid by images of her little office at the top of the shared block where she had spent the previous day and most of the week before. Outer and inner images were both demanding her attention, like the soundtracks of two films playing at the same time.

In the film playing out from the previous days, Alice saw the receptionist in her new serviced offices, who was always ready with a bubbly word or two for everyone. 'Good morning, how are you…

Good weekend… Chilly isn't it?' and the like. She was friendly, quite a chatterbox.

Sitting there from nine to five every day, the receptionist knew what was going on with all the other organizations in the serviced building, a motley mix of small enterprises and charities. She had always had an interest in disability issues and was good friends with one of Alice's board members.

It's good to take an interest in your colleagues' personal lives, to be friendly. But there's a big 'but'! If you become friends, as distinct from being friendly colleagues, know that occasionally you will need to erect a firewall to separate professional and personal lives. Hold some work matters out of the friendship, and some friendship matters out of work. Watch your words. Keep the boundary.

Prompted by something flashing past the window, Alice remembered the critical ('Is that really the best use of your time?') stare of one of the trustees when she had mentioned she would be going to a conference to meet other civil society leaders. But Alice was on it and wanted to be out there.

Her head was spinning with the image of her new office space and the turbulence of her first month. A previous director had jazzed it up by painting two of the walls a sunshine yellow and the team had adorned the space with some colourful posters of nature with aspirational messages. One – vivid green pastures with a winding path leading to sunlit uplands – carried the caption in flowing handwritten script: 'Your actions today will lead you to a better tomorrow.'

It wasn't to Alice's taste, a truism, she thought, but as a team player she didn't want to ruffle feathers, so she let the green cheesiness hang there.

They had all chipped in for their new coffee machine, which had arrived earlier in the week. It whirred and produced an appetising swooshy-gurgling noise. It was like a new friend living in the office to help them get going in the morning and sustain them during the day.

We're sure going to need it, thought Alice as she and Jez opened up the budget spreadsheet.

Good leaders are active players in their own organizational dynamics. They know they are the 'locus of control' so they notice, seek to understand and act as a conscious agent in the system of which they are part. Not at the mercy of events, they actively navigate in the direction they consider is best.

The traces of Alice's dream drifted into her day's reverie. It was one of her repeating nightmares in which she was doing a maths exam but hadn't been to any of the classes (apparently a common nightmare of non-financial specialists).

Office Manager Jez took care of all the practical things needed to keep the charity going, including HR with the help of an external agency. Earlier in the year she had taken on finance too, just after they got the actually-a-bit-too-big-for-them grant from the Big Lottery. But Jez was slowly getting her head around it. It was all good practice for the bookkeeping course she had just started.

'How's it looking?' Alice had said.

'Hmmm… not sure.'

Despite their best efforts to make sense of the numbers for next year, looking at it this way and that, they couldn't see how the numbers could possibly produce a balanced budget. It just didn't add up. But the board seemed to be relaxed about it.

'Am I the only one who doesn't get it? Am I missing something?' she asked Jez, from whom there was no response other than a perplexed smile.

PULLED ALONG BY AN
UNDERCURRENT FROM
ACCOUNTS

They were to meet with Sarah, founder Chair, the following week to prepare for the forthcoming quarterly board meeting, which would be combined with a Christmas drink for volunteers. Keen to make a good first impression, Alice had to get the numbers to add up and deliver the right answer.

Better not to be forever tossed around by the vicissitudes of the day; better to connect to figurative calmer deeper waters than to ride up and down the waves.

An essential skill for any leader is to think for themselves. 'The quality of everything human beings do – everything – depends on the quality of the thinking we do first.'[8]

And so it was, a month into her new job, on her way to a day of mingling, that Alice's recollections of the day before and the passing suburbia blended into an unsettling mind muddle. Her short night and early start, missing her connection and worrying about whether her partner had made it to the nursery with their two-year-old didn't help.

There was something about the freshly jazzed up sunshine yellow walls that had scrambled her brain. Since her first day a month before she had found she couldn't think clearly in the office, a single

---

[8] Nancy Kline *Time to Think: Listening to Ignite the Human Mind* (1999).

room in serviced offices on the outskirts of the town. There was a good view of the car park on one side of the always-busy roundabout and the supermarket on the other. Alice hoped that next year they could find the money to move somewhere bigger and brighter. At interview, the founder Chair had airily pronounced that she didn't see why not. 'Oh yes, we could think about that.'

Hoping to clear their heads, Alice and Jez had popped around the corner to a local café to have another crack at the numbers.

Little things may be just that – little inconsequential things. But they may also be the first sign of something going badly wrong. Notice, make a mental note and then, if there's a second and a third 'little thing', take a closer look. Are these three points lining up, pointing in the same direction? Focus on observable facts, and if you think there's something to it, do something.

Curiously, just at that moment, the train jolted Alice out of her recollections and she saw a First Direct advert whizz past. Direct… director. Tricks of the mind, she thought, as she drifted back a few months to the moment in the interview when she had asked about how they had been managing everything without a director.

Alice remembered the awkwardness in the air as they said, 'Well, yes there was someone who helped out in the office for a while.' They didn't say that they had appointed a first director, but that she had left after a few weeks, having been offered another job. Then they recruited an interim on a part-time, short-term contract, but he also left after a couple of months.

The trustees had changed the job description a bit, renaming the position to 'CEO' and were now recruiting again. Alice was keen to move on in her career and she didn't listen to the little voice fluttering in her ear: 'Look before you leap… look before you leap… look before…' First director? No, actually she was the third.

Listen to what's not said as much as to what is said. Two directors leaving in rapid succession is a red flag and it means that there's something happening beyond what the eye can see – which will soon come into view.

Although it was part-time, Alice had been told at interview that the trustees wanted to make it full-time before too long. The two trustees at interview had seemed nice enough. The voice telling her to grab the chance – her first CEO position after several youth and community jobs that she had fallen into straight from college – shouted louder than the quiet voice telling her that something didn't quite make sense.

She noticed she felt a knot tighten inside her when she thought about meeting the Chair to go through the budget. They had said they should start meeting once a month if they could both make it. This budget meeting was to be the first, and young Alice hoped the Chair would be able to throw some light on the numbers.

'We will soon be arriving at Euston, our last station stop. We apologize for the late running of this service and any inconvenience this may have caused.'

Alice had indeed been inconvenienced.

She thought, *By the time I get there I'll have missed half the morning. I'll miss all the best bits. It's embarrassing turning up late. Maybe I'll give up. Get the handouts afterwards. I just want to get there.*

A FACE To FACE
MEETING

A VIDEO MEETING

Nevertheless, always keen and ever the optimist, she gathered up her stuff and resolved to make the best of the day.

Alice, along with other characters in this unfolding drama, were innocent for a few more moments of how their stories would interweave like skeins of wool.

The pop-up community (is safe)

Having anticipated the flow of events (they were good at that) and having calculated that the end of their session might arrive early, Chris and Sam, the lawyers, had positioned themselves close to the door. They were in pole position as people headed for the exit. Some accepted their offer of handouts while others were distracted by events and were looking the other way.

As he joined the flow of animated conference-goers escorted to the relative safety of the street by yet more 'Here to Helpers' (whose yellow emergency high-viz tabards clashed horribly with the tangerine T-shirts), Bob couldn't resist the temptation. 'Told you,' he said. 'I knew there was something up. No one else noticed.'

He looked around but pink-hair Rose, who had been by his side just a second ago, had been swept away in the flood and Bob found he was instead addressing a soberly dressed woman, carrying a sensible bag.

Upfront as ever, Bob ventured, 'How come no one said anything? It smelled like burnt chips.'

'I knew something wasn't right,' said sensible Grace, 'but I was too wrapped up with what the presenter was saying to notice, like the rest of us.'

The smilingly polite servers, as instructed, had readily abandoned the coffee and pastries, glad of the distraction. As Grace, Bob and a few hundred leaders tumbled their way along the evacuation route to the Assembly Area, the coffee urn burbled as if saying, 'Something's brewing... something's brewing...'

As Tara was swept along by the crowd, an image of rising wild waters flashed in front of her. *That dream, that dream, it's that stupid dream again!* Always different (a sea, a lake, a river) but always the same – suddenly rising waters heading towards her from nowhere, and always ending with a gasp and heart-pumping relief on waking.

For many years I had a recurring dream of rising waters. There were many different scenarios but always the same sudden overwhelm that woke me. I was going through a process of active self-reflection and understood this to be the opening of unconscious layers. After some while they slowed, stopped and now occur only occasionally.

Spilling onto the street, conference-goers, initially irritated by the interruption to their noble deliberations, were now behaving like excited children let out of school early.

When they had signed in earlier, conference attendees had already started melding as a community. Now facing the common existential threat of fire made them a sort of pop-up civil society community with total strangers becoming instant best friends of the day.

Excited huddles formed in the street, which was blessed by unseasonably clement weather – indeed this was the warmest November day since records began. In this unforeseen moment, squeezed onto the pavement to avoid the midday traffic, their chatter became at once more convivial and more intense. For conference-goers this was an unexpected opportunity for more networking, and for the servers a welcome opportunity for not working.

Tara was happy to find she and Robin had landed on the same bit of pavement, as it happened, right next to a revolving street poster that at that very moment declared: 'What's in your inbox today?' with a picture of a delighted recipient winning a prize of a world cruise. *Chance would be a fine thing*, thought Tara, *all I get in mine are annoying late-night work emails. Each one lands like a poke in the ribs, which is not what you need before bedtime.*

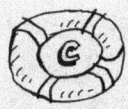

Especially when times are tough, don't leave the email or social media doors wide open all day. Try letting it be known that, to manage your attention, you process your emails twice a day: mid-morning and late afternoon. Or try once a day, or once or twice a week. Be kind to yourself and *never* open your emails late in the evening – screens and emails, irritating or exciting, do not deliver a good night's sleep.

Right next to her, Tara saw pink-hair Rose and recalled having seen her across a crowded room and, in the spirit of the pop-up civil society community, greeted her with a breezy 'this is all a bit different, isn't it?' 'Yes, I'm glad it didn't happen in the first workshop about youth media,' said Rose.

A mysterious hand guided Bob and Grace to a space on the pavement, just a few steps away from the revolving poster, which was now playfully asking: 'Is it me you're looking for?' alongside a sketch of a Lionel Richie lookalike candidate in a smart suit, smiling enticingly in front of an interview panel.

Magic was in the air and a few moments later those who been strangers were now drawn into a jostling connected pop-up community.

Arriving in a fluster after her irritating journey, Alice was perplexed yet relieved to be greeted not by an empty foyer and sessions behind closed doors as she had expected, but by a street full of animated conversations. For a moment she hovered uneasily as a lone outsider, hoping to become an insider.

Then from somewhere in the jostle there appeared a voice: 'I have the lawyer handout.' An arm appeared out of the melee and handed a note to a surprised Alice. From somewhere she heard 'Is this what you're looking for? You need it more than me. Read it, think about it. Do it.'

With handout in hand and now more curious than ever, Alice was glad to have been embraced by the spirit of generosity. *What a very puzzling place this is*, thought Alice.

Alice was even more surprised when Bob ventured 'We were just getting to the good bit,' instantly promoting her from outsider to insider. 'That lawyer was going to say something about doing good communication with your team and how the law might protect you when the sugar hits the fan. I need one of those handouts.'

'Is this what you're looking for... and what have I missed?' Alice was now in the flow of civil conversations, hearing about the noble struggles of other leaders and contributing her own story of new job, unfathomable budget and being the third director, not the first. This community of like-minded, open-minded and engaging people intent on creating a more civil kind of society is what she had hoped to find, and she had landed slap-bang in the middle of it.

Thinking that she should try to bump into Sarah, she preferred the company of these enthusiasts. *It's good to be here*, she thought, and her thoughts shone through.

Meanwhile, Sarah, having been carrried from the building by the crowd, had found herself in the company of an earnest besuited man who, without so much as a how do you do, launched into telling her about the many charities he was chairing and now, having his house in the country, thought it was time to 'give something back'.

So taken was she by his stories that she didn't extract herself to approach the young Alice, who she spotted in animated conversation the other side of the crowd. But they did manage to exchange a fleeting glance and waved awkwardly at each other.

Overcome your resistance to initiating a difficult conversation as if you were summoning all your reserves of courage to do bungee jumping. Bungee jumping isn't essential to the health of your organization, but courageous conversations are.

And so it was, in a London street on an unseasonably warm November day by a revolving sign that was now declaring: 'Anything is possible' alongside an image of a long and winding road, that many wisdoms were circulating and many stories were unfolding.

Imran (passes by)

Doing his best to squeeze through the crowd unnoticed, Imran was on his way back to his office after a lunch meeting with other investment managers. The buzz of the animated conversations of the pop-up community tempted him to linger a few moments, catching a few phrases here and there. He was intrigued by what he heard.

These words were a far cry from his harsh world of hedge funds, investments and the like. Imran was drawn onwards and, after a few moments, far beyond the crowd as he approached the familiar marble world of his city office, he came across a *Big Issue* seller. Imran passed him by most days, but today there seemed to have a different air about him, something less of a stranger. Wondering whether this might a lucky day, investor Imran stepped over his awkwardness and bought a copy to read on his commute.

Little did he know then that 12 months hence he would be looking back at this moment as his first faltering steps on a new path.

You never know who you are standing next to. You will never know what harsh or happy stories they have hidden, until you press the pause button on your own stuff and get into conversation with them.

Time for lunch

Their pop-up exchanges continued for a while longer, until a ripple passed through the crowd saying that the coast was clear, so the pop-up community knew it was time for lunch. Several rumours were circulating about what had happened, the favourite being that there had indeed been a fire, in the kitchen right next to the 'Don't Drift Into Crisis' workshop. How fitting. A handywoman with a screwdriver had fixed the wiring fault, which was duly declared safe.

No one saw that high above and tucked between the towering office blocks there was a heavy cloud, drifting in the direction of the conference. Intent as they were on their more immediate concerns, no one connected that darkening sky with the chill wind whistling around the corner and the likelihood of trouble ahead.

As hungry souls tried to slide their way to the head of the lunch queue while trying not to be seen as pushy, the stream of delegates passed by the warming log fire video above the reception desk.

The servers, having been glad of the interruption to their routine, were now back at their stations. Following its collective twitching nose, the crowd surged past a sector notable who was more interested in her earnest conversation with the Chair of the charity regulator about whistleblowing than she was in her free lunch.

Engaged in animated conversation, she was espousing the benefits of having a full set of organizational policies, which she opined was an essential prerequisite of a healthy well-prepared organization.

'If you don't have a full set of up-to-date and approved policies, you're going to end up in deep water one day. I've seen it all too often. They're like a lifeline that should always be ready but are rarely needed,' she said. Yes indeed, how true.

The crowd passed by the worthy policy conversations, more intent on the immediate goodies on offer, not aware of the gems they were missing, nor of the challenges that lay ahead.

Like a life jacket, a full set of policies and procedures are not urgent until the day you need them urgently. At that moment it's too late. So start right now to write or review a full range of policies so you can stay afloat when the flood waters rise. Here's a start: compassionate leave, complaints, disciplinary, exit, health and safety, induction, social media, maternity and paternity leave, sick leave, time off in lieu, trustees' expenses, volunteers... They should not gather dust on a shelf but be live documents that will be lifesavers in wild waters. *Endnote³*

There were voices in the air – 'remember these things… remember these things… remember…' above the clatter of the lunch queue, but few were listening, being overtaken by more immediate concerns.

Into wild waters

The lunch experience was a familiar mix of trying to find a chair and, when none was to be found, of balancing animated conversation with forkfuls of food. Achieving this feat was an essential social art well practised by some, apparently less so by others. *Why don't they teach you this stuff at school?* pondered Alice.

The afternoon passed uneventfully enough, offering food for thought that some found compelling and others less so; all but a 'sorry-got-to-go' few headed dutifully to the closing plenary. Although some conference stalwarts remained, for many the affairs of the day were fading fast as the everyday busy-nesses of life were calling – a school meeting, choir, football, pub, a tsunami of emails.

That's the price you pay for a day out of the office, thought Robin. *It's the same as VAT – you have to add a couple of hundred emails and voice messages to the conference fee.* Neatly unfolding his recently acquired folding bike (his wife said it was the healthy option), he spotted the cloud, now a few shades darker. *Hmm, there may be trouble ahead.*

Securing his helmet – you never know what might be heading your way – he waved farewell to Rose and Bob. Smiling, they were so engaged in chatter about something apparently important that with a screech of tyres they were nearly hit by a passing truck. 'Oops, didn't see that one coming,' joked Bob as they raced towards the approaching number 42 bus.

Seeing this little drama play out as she buttoned her coat against the early evening chill, Sarah's sparkly hat caught the blue light of the passing fire engine racing to quench flames somewhere.

Alice and Grace found that by happy chance they were heading for the same tube station for their northbound trains. They exchanged various nuggets from the business of the day, enjoyed the Christmas decorations ('They're putting these up earlier every year, aren't they?') and Alice admitted to having mopped up a few handfuls of Celebrations to take home to her wife as a sweet but inadequate compensation for her early rising to drive Alice to the station.

As they descended from fading evening light into the underground labyrinth, Alice heard a dog barking behind them, an unexpected sound in city streets. It sounded like the kind of warm friendly dog that you might come across in a park one day.

Having said farewell to Alice, Grace was now alone in the crowded tube for a few minutes more and caught herself recalling what she had shared with Tara that morning. 'Chair... 26 years... what will we do when he goes... some trustees haven't been to a meeting for a while... a few do all the work... that new trustee has started pushing his weight around... have to think about that... we don't have a plan...'

A nagging disquiet rattled around in her as the doors opened at Euston and she soon heard the familiar announcement: 'See it. Say it. Sorted.' Good idea.

The security advice that you will hear if you use public transport in London – 'See it. Say it. Sorted.' – translates well into the daily lives of good leaders. Keep your eyes open so you 'see it', 'say it' to a trusted someone (to stop it rattling around your head space) and start getting it sorted by deciding what one action you will take to get it 'sorted'. And make it 'SNAPPY' (see below).

And so it was that each innocently travelled home – to go deeper into their wild waters stories.

SNAPPY

Red flags, like headaches, are useful signals. These triggers tell us something, but they are only one part of the story – we are the other. Unless we notice them and do something, red flags will wave more wildly as we head for those wild waters.

As you may know, crocodiles wait for their lunch in calmer waters at the end of the rapids. How much better it is to avoid that crocodile kind of 'snappy' by Stopping, Noticing, Analysing, Planning and Proceeding when you see danger ahead. Avoid being lunch for the hungry beast.

Yes, *you* make it SNAPPY. It starts with *you*, because as the very best leader you can be, *you* are your own locus of control.

S is for STOP

Although as Chairs, board members and CEOs we are (more or less) actively engaged in our organizations, there are things we cannot or choose not to see. Red flags sit in our blind spots.

It's natural to avoid the unpleasant. Not paying attention to difficult stuff is commonplace. The bad news is that avoidance serves to postpone, not resolve. So, as coach, I support learning how to develop better skills for facing the unpleasant – and that starts with stopping.

We may be just too frightened of what we may find if we lift the bonnet. If we blindly carry on and hope it will all work out, sooner or later we will drift into choppy and maybe raging wild waters.

S is for Stop... Interrupt your daily pattern. Replace your habit of noticing rarely and replace it with a habit of noticing often.

Stopping does not have to mean spending a month in a wilderness cave pondering the meaning of life. Stopping can be much simpler than that, much closer to home – a walk alone or with a friend, time sitting by a river, 20 minutes at your desk looking out of the window, putting pen to paper and writing what flows out of the end of the pen. Any space with minimal external stimuli will do.

An hour or two with a coach is one way to stop. Sharing your story with an attentive, compassionate deep listener can help you to interrupt your habit.

Stopping comes more naturally to some than others, but for all of us, as the noise of external stimuli around us decreases, we have taken the first step on a path of discovery and towards resolution.

N is for NOTICE

Some of the red flags we may notice are visible to anyone who cares to look. Some examples: without explanation, the board has recently started to hold closed sessions without the CEO at the end of each meeting. The CEO, who has consistently responded promptly to mails and messages, is now responding erratically. Maybe the new Chair no longer meets with the CEO every month but announces that a call a few days before board meetings will suffice. Perhaps a couple of trustees have stopped attending meetings.

Some red flags are known only to you and your confidants: your sleep patterns have been disturbed for the last couple of months, you are feeling morose, you have a constant tightness in your back. A health issue that troubled you years ago is reappearing; a persistent mild headache is getting you down. You notice you are waking too early with a sense of foreboding and some days you struggle to get out of bed.

These and many more red flags, helpful triggers, are waiting to guide you on your way.

You are not in wild waters yet but maybe the change in the river flow, a plume of spray ahead or a distant rumble tell you that you are drifting towards a waterfall.

It may be that a single red flag, whether visible to all or known only to you, is not significant. But together with other observations and over time they may spell trouble; watch the whole film, not just one screenshot.

A is for ACCEPT, APPRECIATE, ANALYSE

You have pressed the stop button and noticed. A is for accept, appreciate and analyse, or any of these in any order.

Take what you notice and break it down into its essential features. How long has this been happening, is it always the same, is it around the same person, when does it happen? Stand back from individual facts to see connections, discern patterns and flow over time. Sense into it to discover what it could mean.

You can do this when walking, or writing alone, but having someone outside the dynamic to walk with, literally and/or figuratively, can help. Their attention, care and deep listening can help you unravel, disentangle, make sense and understand. Your first thought on waking up could be a clue.

You may well not come up with an explanation of which you feel certain, but you may well come up with a working hypothesis that is good enough to get on and to make a plan.

P is for PLAN

'Plan' is not a complex process over months. The plan is more likely to be an emerging sense of direction with the impetus to move and one or two first actions.

Just get moving. Take the next action. Bring it to the next Chair/CEO meeting, speak with the Finance Committee Chair, raise it at the next Chair/Vice-Chair meeting or check out the working hypothesis with a senior colleague.

P is for PROCEED

'Snapy' doesn't work – it has to be 'snappy'. To fulfil the potential of your stopping, noticing, analysing and planning, you have to 'p' for proceed, actually do something, say something, be an agent in your own future. Actually take the first step. Do it.

One step will generate a second and a third. A way ahead will start opening up.

YOU

You, a good leader who cares about the future of humanity, are at the heart of things. This is equally true for leaders of a household name international company as for a local community charity. Being at the heart of things means that you own and exercise the locus of control. Fully embrace the 'Y' and make it SNAPPY.

And when that's done, repeat: Stop, Notice, Analyse, Plan and Proceed (yes, You).

Chapter 2
A WILD WEDNESDAY, ONE YEAR LATER

GET THROUGH IT, SURVIVE

We find our characters feeling alone,
each in the depths of their wild waters. It's a desperate time,
but even in this dark place there's hope…

OUT OF
YOUR DEPTH

'The one thing you can't take away from me is the way I choose to respond to what you do to me. The last of one's freedoms is to choose one's attitude in any given circumstance.'[9]

What'sUp

Once upon a time there was a true story.

Good leaders were chattering, east, west, north, south throughout the land. By mail, phone, conferencing platforms, social media and more, a cacophony of messages tumbled through the ether.

Exchanges flashed here and there, Chair to CEO, CEO to executive team, CEO to board member, within executive teams and all other possible permutations of chatter on the airwaves and also face to face. There were calm exchanges and there were shouty ones too, and that signalled crisis for some.

'It was okay to start with.' 'Something's changed over the last few weeks hasn't it?'

---

[9] Viktor Frankl, referring to his experience of Second World War concentration camps. *Man's Search for Meaning: An Introduction to Logotherapy* (1984).

'What the hell was all that about…?' 'She shouldn't have just pushed you out of the way like that.'

'He's just not up to it…' 'Why don't we give him a chance.' 'No way, he's had enough chances already…'

'Did you see that funny look she gave me?' 'There's definitely something weird happening, don't you think?'

'Why don't you say something?' 'Why don't *you*?'

'What's happening?' 'I don't know, I don't get it.'

'We've got to do something.' 'Who's "we"?'

'They used the work bankcard to buy coffee.' 'What! Really?' 'Okay, he paid it back, but still, it's against the rules.' 'Yes, but does it matter?'

'Maybe it'll sort itself out.' 'Time will tell.' 'Let's wait and see.'

Robin (is awake on gardening leave)

Shaking but not able to scream, Robin was suddenly wide awake. This was real. Someone coming at him. Attack. Heart racing. Breathing fast, huh-a-huh-a-huh.

Slowly the dark night dawned on him. A nightmare. Not real. Trying to make sense of the jumble, all he could remember was his face being pushed into something. A pillow? A wall? An invisible force pressed him down. Couldn't breathe.

A dread of suffocation had dragged him up from the depths into the dead of night. The cold green eye of the clock told him that it was 4am. Like yesterday and many nights before that, he awoke feeling that he was all alone, despite the steady breathing of his wife.

His night demons were calling on him again. In the dark, his own panicked breath was short and tense. The passing moment of relief that the worst hadn't happened gave way to his waking into another nightmare, a real one. Dawn was many long hours away.

The harsh truth crawled its way through his body, a tense malevolence seeping through every muscle. Alone in the dark, Robin recalled the moment nearly eight weeks ago when he had just been suspended from work. 'Gardening leave' they called it. The Chair had told him that complaints had been received that had to be taken seriously, so there would have to be a thorough investigation. He had said he wanted to deal with this matter 'expeditiously' and that Robin would be suspended for six weeks.

Six weeks. The number was easy to remember because he had started work at the hospice exactly six years ago as deputy, then was promoted to CEO. Now eight weeks had dragged past.

After weeks of waiting for the phone to ring or an email to land, he eventually heard that an independent investigator had been appointed. Robin had an email from her last week in which she crisply and courteously she said she would get back to him soon about next steps. Then silence.

What's happening? He couldn't make sense of it. He heard nothing, except the incessant drone of worry. It was dark, no noise from the street, the world slept. Awake alone. This was bad enough during the day but overwhelming at night.

Not wanting to wake his wife, he lay motionless while his mind raced round a track with no exit. Circular thoughts, round and round. No way out. Head was hot, feet were cold. Touching but not falling into the sleep he craved, he shifted this way and that way with no way to turn.

His wife was with him all the way, but she needed her sleep too. Hoping she might wake to offer some comfort but knowing he must leave her be, he crumpled himself out of bed and groped his way across their familiar room. Front room alone, silent, dark but for faint street light filtering. Kitchen, cat in the corner stirring as if it might be food time already.

Inner voice: *Can't stand, can't sit, can't lie, no good, I have to get out of here. Out, yes, fresh air, breathe. Nature.* Robin loved nature. *Space. Fresh air. Get out.*

The cold damp autumn air brushed his face, fresh and biting. Robin walked, alone in the street but for a fox limping under the hedge of number 42. All houses and flats dark. They all slept. 'Okay for them.' Towards the canal he passed only one light up on the second floor and wondered – a child awake, someone working late, starting early, or another sleepless soul?

Most of the world, most of the time is awake. Of those for whom it is night, around a third of the global population, some are awake at the same moment as you are and may be grappling with their demons. You may feel despair but remember that you are not alone. You are in a community of sleepless ones. *Endnote⁹*

Away from the street lights, he was drawn to the little piece of nature not so far from his sleeping wife for whom he had left a note.

He headed for nature and came to their canal, in sunnier days a favourite haunt for evening strolls but now sombre, it was at once inviting and dreadful.

For many decades I ignored my inner voice constantly calling me to go into nature. I was always too busy, too distracted, too hectic. Thankfully, the trees are patient and were still there when I was eventually ready to follow my inner voice. 'Go there,' my friend said.

Sitting on the bench, Robin couldn't bear the ache of dread in every part of him, inside and out. It was hours until dawn. Cold penetrating. A voice told him he could find peace in the watery dark depths. 'Go on' – and at the same instant the fresh air told him no.

I wonder if this triggers painful memories for you. It does for me. I remember a dark moment in the small hours walking by the Thames to sit by the local church to find solace. The river waters beckoned me – what an instant relief it would be – but the thought of those close to me held me back. Now, decades later, that same stretch of river is a happy wild swimming playground for me. How things change.

He saw the silhouetted trees against the night-grey skyline and thought of his wife, and the note.

After how much time he didn't know, good fortune passed by in the form of an early morning dog walker. A cheery 'You alright there?' was thrown his way, of the sort you might hear from a young shop assistant, but this one was tinged with real concern. Hearing no reply, the dog walker said again, 'Are you alright?' He was surmising what Robin knew too well. Robin was not alright. He was on the edge.

But this momentary lifeline, as a lifering tossed into the water, was enough for Robin to pause and think again. His inner voice told him, *Hold on.* So he did.

He noticed the trees, the grass, the lush nature he longed for. The abundance had always been there but for a moment he saw it anew. He knew they were his own words while imagining he heard them say, 'It's okay, we're here. We will wait for you.' *Nature is like that*, he thought. *Patient, no hurry.* Endnote[10]

Trees have been there since the start of things; a forever lifeline for those of us who care to reach for it. Robin did.

After the passing of some hours he had torn up the note, thrown it in the recycling and had fed the cat. Now he was waiting for his wife to wake.

Tara (is hit by a truck)

That very same Wednesday, 12 hours later and some miles away, Tara was collapsed on a sofa, beating herself up for not having seen it coming. The events of last week had hit her like a truck. Crash.

Trucks happen, bricks happen. Occasionally life flows along easily. Sometimes it does not. Commenting on his being sacked by Apple at the age of 30, Steve Jobs said, 'Sometimes life is going to hit you in the head with a brick.' His 2005 Stanford Commencement Address continued, 'I'm convinced that the only thing that kept me going was that I loved what I did... You've got to find what you love... Don't let the noise of others' opinions drown out your own inner voice'.[10]

It was ever thus. Our lives are a constant roller coaster of joys and sorrows as we struggle to make the most of our brief sojourn on planet Earth by getting through the daily round of shopping, caring for family, fixing stuff, finding our socks and other tasks great and small. Stuff happens, and when it hurts that is not an obstacle but part of our way. Noting outer voices but responding to our inner voice will get us through.

---

[10] Steve Jobs' 2005 Stanford Commencement Address https://bit.ly/42B-fzmx from minute 8.

There had been a private board meeting earlier last week and the next day Tara was due to have her regular meeting with the now not-so-new Chair. A few months previously, the board had started having special meetings in private; Tara hadn't asked why nor attached too much significance to it. She hadn't seen that red flag flying.

The board holding meetings in private might be a red flag. But it might not be. There should be a stated purpose of which the executive is aware, along with appropriate feedback and a record made afterwards. If not, questions should be asked...

Tara still remembered the previous Chair who had appointed her nine years previously; a comfortable relationship, everything had rolled along nicely.

But this new one... oh dear. For many months now she had been polite and patient with him, making an effort to get on. Although everything had seemed fine to start with, he was now proving himself to be better at speaking than listening. She carried their relationship as a heavy burden, and she was only just managing.

At her regular meeting with the Chair two weeks previously (now shifted to Wednesday evenings, 'To fit in with his tight schedule,' said his PA), Tara was all set to discuss the forthcoming volunteer celebration event and plans for next year's anniversary. But the Chair had come with other matters to put on the table. She had walked into the room to find that he was flanked by two other trustees, whom the now not-so-new Chair had drafted on to the board. She remembered the gut-wrenching feeling as she saw the awkward intensity in their eyes.

'Some board members have made complaints,' said the Chair bluntly. 'We'll tell you what we can,' which turned out to be not very much. She couldn't find the words to reply, not least because there was not much to respond to (who complained, about what and when). Some 30 minutes later with insides in a knot she staggered downstairs, gripping the handrail, and into the dark street. She had been holding on for so long and finally all that had been hidden had now crashed onto the table.

Her recent appraisal had gone well enough. But she now remembered that the trustee who had done it (Head of HR in a big corporate) had still not written it up. Tara had assumed she was just too busy but vaguely wondered if there was more to it.

Yes, there could be an innocent explanation for a performance review not being written up – the person who did the review is busy, unwell, on holiday or distracted by family matters. But it could also be the case that there's some avoidance going on, something difficult to deal with, so writing up the appraisal is parked in the too-difficult corner. Too hot to handle, it's avoided. Spot that red flag.

A few weeks previously the HR subcommittee had made salary recommendations for all staff but had apparently forgotten about hers; generously, she surmised they would get round to doing hers later.

She tried to make sense of it but couldn't. Tara's generous speculations had turned out to be hopelessly naïve, the truth being altogether more sinister.

An inevitable part of crisis is not knowing. Conversations are happening behind your back, over your head, under the table, not with you. As you know only some bits of the story, you can't make sense of it. The fog of war hangs around you and you can't see through it.

Tara knew this place. It had been like this years ago in the centuries-old country house and museum when a polarising debate about the relative merits of conservation and restoration, and between preserving the old and hunger for the new, had got massively out of hand.

She had suffered, and after these many years she thought she had got over it, but in fact had just got used to carrying the burden like a loaded backpack. And now over the last year she had been carrying new burdens, and although she had tried and tried to work things through, she had felt that same creeping physical tension in her back and her belly screaming at her as she headed home two weeks previously.

The doctor had signed her off for three weeks. ('Work-related stress,' she said. 'You're not the first and you won't be the last, you need some time away.')

Crumpled in slumber on the afternoon sofa, drained of all energy, falling into an uneasy day-sleep, Tara's pains were now pulling her up and out. 'Can't sleep but I don't want to be awake either.' Tears were trying to surface but were trapped in her shoulders and needed human company to draw them out. Her solitary sofa was no place to weep.

With our minds clouded by emotion, we can't think clearly and our clouded thinking can produce unwise behaviour.

Allowing ourselves some emotional release, like washing a dirty windscreen, is one way of clearing away the accumulated debris that's clouding our vision. This human release valve is best triggered not when we are alone but with another human being alongside us, a step behind. Allowing 'sufficient emotional release to restore thinking' is one of the ten components of the Thinking Environment. *Endnote*

This was not yet a new dawn in her story, but a misty November dusk.

As well as the unspecified complaints, they were 'losing confidence' in her, they had said. They appreciated all her good work over nine years but now the environment was changing fast. 'Surely you can see that?' they said. 'We expect you to produce a plan of how you could improve your performance.'

Every month she would have to go through it with a recent arrival on the board, a self-made local businessman who was earning himself a reputation for never taking no for an answer. She had just about managed to hold back tears of rage and hurt.

With tension like some alien creature crawling over her, Tara heaved herself off the sofa. She hadn't had a proper night's sleep for two weeks; her unconscious had been digging at her and now her conscious mind was desperately trying to work out what on earth had been happening. Over the last days she had found herself collapsing onto the sofa, falling into a dead-weight sleep during the afternoon. She wanted water but couldn't move.

Her partner was at work and the kids were staying over with friends. She was on her own.

The radio offered little comfort: 'It's 4 o'clock… this is the news. The leader of the opposition is demanding an inquiry…' The words were drowned out by the noise in Tara's head. And anyway, she didn't care what the inquiry was about. Same old, same old. But she did care about trying to make sense of recent events. Inquiry. Indeed.

She couldn't raise herself off the sofa and couldn't stop her mind wandering back over the events of the last year. She remembered the conversation at the conference a year ago with that gentleman who had offered her a chair and the kind woman who had listened so deeply, as if she was genuinely interested. Maybe she had been.

Now, a year later, she was finding out what she had known then but hadn't recognized. She didn't then, but now she had time to think, indeed too much.

She thought of her mum and dad, Asian and Irish, who had chosen 'Tara', which had meaning in both of their cultures. What would they have done? She wondered how much of her personal history had called her to work in the heritage sector; perhaps it was some roundabout way of connecting with her own family heritage?

Dozing off again, the noise of traffic and piercing sirens faded and Tara found herself outside. Floating in her inner world, she saw herself outside the room, above the street, seeing herself as part of a bigger picture, not at the centre of it but as one player in a grand drama.

Four and half billion years after Earth was created and some decades before selfies were invented, astronauts turned the camera round to snap a picture of planet Earth. Thanks to them, we can now see our planet as a 'pale blue dot' in the whole solar system. Holding this in mind may help us to see our daily struggles in perspective as a tiny human dot in our team, organizational, sectoral and universal system. We are players in the grand scheme of things. May we play our part well.

Then the damp November mist closed in again and she was again trapped in her unwanted wanderings and wonderings about what had come to pass. The sofa, which once upon a time had been a place to sip wine and enjoy TV, had now become a padded cell from which Tara couldn't escape.

The radio, talking to itself in the kitchen, chattered on incessantly, faintly reaching Tara through the half-open door. The chatter gave her some comfort, but she couldn't concentrate for more than a few moments. Then she heard something about 'do one thing... just one thing'.

For many of us, including me, working to support civil society, on top of earning money, can give us a sense of meaning and the satisfaction of creating a society that's sustainable, decent and just; it's a noble way of earning a living. But it's tough as we plough through our meetings, sending emails, making calls, writing reports.

Stuff happens: money is tight, it's hard to recruit, a loved one is seriously ill, the IT system is playing up, then comes a grievance from senior team members, a complaint about the conduct of a board member, another resignation without adequate explanation, an illness, a nuclear argument, a relationship crash and more broken nights. We battle on with a mix of ego-driven determination, a resolve to deliver on our promises to be a good leader.

Then comes the day when it's all too much. We can't carry on. The burden is too much to carry alone and we need someone to walk alongside (and a close half-step behind) us. That person helps us find our strength to figure out ways to face and fix what's going on and also to reconnect to the joy and meaning of our work.

The nudge to do just one thing got to her. Not two things, not everything, but just one thing. Do it. Start with one step. All mixed up with her circular thinking about the events of the last year, Tara resolved to lift herself off the sofa. That was one thing. Now, do just one more thing.

She managed to make it all the way to the kitchen, turned on the kettle and found a tea bag, milk, sugar and a cup, made herself a cup of tea, donned a woolly hat and stood on their little balcony with its boxes of drooping geraniums. How bright they had been just a couple of months ago. 'Yes I can. Just one thing. They're such a mess. Tidy them for winter.'

And so she did. An hour later the bin was full of dying foliage and the plant boxes were safely tucked away from the coming cold.

In her depression and anxiety, having successfully achieved this simple act felt as if she had scaled a mountain. Encouraged by her big success, Tara managed a passing thought that she might even see them bloom again the next summer.

With a hint of a smile inside and another tea in hand, back on the sofa but now sitting up, she had no idea of what would happen next. Read, check her emails again, again and yet again to see if there was anything from work. The tea was warming, and above the rumble of rush-hour traffic she heard the wail of a distant police siren as she waited for her partner to return home to tell him of her success on the balcony.

Tara felt a hint of hope. All was not lost. One year from now…

Don't just lie there, do something. If you feel low, morose and anxious (it happens, I know), will yourself to do something, however seemingly insignificant. Make tea, empty the dishwasher, walk to the shop, buy bread. If you are feeling stronger, buy a new watchstrap (that worked for me), get your hair done, take your coat to the drycleaners. Do a small thing to give you a sense of achievement and nudge you out of your lethargy.

> This small step may also help you to become aware of whether or not you need more substantial help in the form of professional guidance.

Grace (get up, stand up)

Grace felt a glimmer of relief as she realized that the week was two days gone with three to go; then the weekend. Her nights hadn't been getting any better. Like now, she often woke with a tensing back pain a couple of hours after midnight, but this night she had made it all the way to 4am.

Sleeping, dreaming, falling in and out, turbulence in mind. *Why did we hang about so long? We should have got on with getting a new Chair ages ago... And we've never had a Vice-Chair, never needed one... It's all my fault.* Repetitive thinking swirled inside her like a whirlpool.

They had known for ages that their Chair of 25, now 26 years kept saying he was going to retire (grandchildren, garden and the like). He prevaricated, not being able to say goodbye, so Grace raised it many times, and when it seemed no one was listening, just got on with other urgent matters. The Chair's impending retirement was ignored until it was urgent. Very urgent. And when the moment of his last but one board meeting came, they were caught unawares even though they could have easily seen it coming. There was a vacuum around the board table. Nature abhors a vacuum and so did the board table, and that vacuum was soon filled.

Grace's partner always slept like a rock, didn't hear her moaning; a mortar attack wouldn't rouse him. Just as well.

She had tried all sorts of ways of calming herself in the small hours and had found out the hard way that for her, maybe for others too, watching films and listening to the radio were stimulating, not sleep-inducing. As had become her custom during these troubled nights, she tried to summon up the few drops of willpower she could find and eased herself silently out of the bed.

If you wake and sleep won't return, experiment to discover your own best way to bring back slumber.

Too much external stimulus won't help, like bright lights or TV. Think different: if you are learning a language, listen to the radio in that language and your brain may quickly declare defeat ('too difficult, okay you win, switch off'). Maybe the soft voice of a spiritual teacher speaking simply and slowly may do it for you. The sound of gentle waves on the beach, an easy-to-read book, breathing exercises, sleep stories, calming apps...

Try not accepting your insomnia lying down. Get up, sit comfortably, light a candle. Experiment to find what works.

Camomile, candlelight, armchair, write. *Better to get up than lie down,* Grace thought.

She took her pen and lots of scrap paper and started to dump whatever was rumbling around her head. Grace had tried silent prayer, meditation and simply gazing at the candle but none of these cunning tactics worked as well as taking the pen in hand and allowing it to flow.

She had a pile of scrap sheets of A4 that she had accumulated for this very purpose; her husband, snoring loudly a few steps away, graciously called them her 'crap paper'.

A stream of consciousness, a flood with no filter spilling through the pen did the work. She held it but let it go its own way, so even rude words that she would never allow herself to utter during the day, and certainly not at church, found their way out.

If you wake with words rumbling inside your head, then get them out of there and onto paper.

Get up, sit up in a comfy chair. Hold a pen. Scrap paper works better than new paper because it says to you that you can write any old stuff that comes out, no need to write fancy words and whole sentences. Let the pen write what it will.

As the words pour onto the page, let the anger come, the fear, the confusion, peppered with expletives, whatever comes.

After a while there may come a moment when you notice that a nugget of truth has just landed, some words that carry some weight; it stands out and rings true. Pause. Ponder. On that scrappy paper there may be a gem, guiding you to action to find a way through (for me it often lands between page eight and ten).

Words landed on the page, not in straight lines, which was her everyday way, but in a contorted jumble all over the place, up, down and all around. No time limit or other constraint for this release and she had enough (s)crap paper to keep her going all night if she needed. But so long would not be needed.

The words on the page shouted at her not just for being patient, but way too patient and understanding. She was kind and was ready to see the other side of the argument, but the pen told her she had left it too long, she had given her patience, understanding and generosity too much of a free rein. 'Why didn't you challenge them?' the pen demanded. 'They thought I'd fix everything. But I was busy with other stuff, looking the other way.'

As the pen landed on page eight, it scrawled, 'Stand up to him, be as big as you are.' And again, 'Stand up to him, be as big as you are. Stand up to him. Stand up, stand up to that board member who jumped in so quickly to fill the vacuum when the Chair left.'

The pen dug deeper into the paper, but who cares, she mused; it's from the recycling bin. This was the obvious truth that had been lurking inside her. With camomile, calm and candlelight, now was her truth's moment to make an appearance.

My page-eight-to-ten moment of truth was that I would suggest at our meeting the next morning, by then only a few hours away, that the Chair and I as Vice-Chair would swap positions for six months. I was up for the challenge of chairing and he was ready to take a step back. A few hours later we met and he agreed. The arrangement worked.

Landing on these words brought Grace some calm and she felt the tightness in her shoulders letting go. She closed her eyes.

Other forms of freewriting are available. Try 'exploratory writing' (six minutes to respond to a prompt question)[11] and writing three 'morning pages' every day.[12]

After a fitful night and too little sleep, Grace was jumped awake by the alarm. 'What's that about!' she groaned. 'You can't sleep and then the alarm drills a hole in your head.'

When her pulse returned to nearly normal and with heavy eyes creaking open, she found herself humming. 'Get up, stand up, stand up for your rights.' That's it. She heard her own words for the second time and now in the warm light of day they had a firm resolve to them.

'I'm going to stand up to him. Maybe his heart's in the right place but his behaviour is just not acceptable. There's out of order stuff happening. Having got himself appointed Acting Chair, now he's got one of the other board members as his right-hand man and another as a right-hand woman, while the others just sit on their hands. I'm the CEO and I have to do something; it's for me to act,

---

[11] Alison Jones *Exploratory Writing: Everyday Magic for Life and Work* (2023).
[12] Julia Cameron *The Artist's Way* (1995).

it's my job. I'm going to get passive trustees onside; they're decent and they think straight but they're hiding.'

With this newfound resolve she sat at the same kitchen table, now not with the scraps that had helped her in the night, but her proper work to-do list notepad. She made a plan, at first capturing what she needed to do, the calls (including to her friend running a B Corp who certainly knew what day of the week it was), the emails, and the rest, then writing numbers by each one, 1, 2, 3, so she knew where to start. She was so tired that she needed her 1, 2, 3 prop to help her get through the day, rather like painting by numbers delivers you a picture.

Bomb-proof husband wandered into the kitchen, unaware of the turbulence of the night.

'I'm going to stand up to him,' said Grace graciously and firmly. I'm not putting up with this anymore. I've had enough.' How good it was to speak it out. Speaking out strengthened her resolve.

Telling yourself that you are going to do something is a good start, and telling someone else you will do it is even better. Speaking it out, hearing your words, not inside your head but outside, and knowing that they are now also in another's, will strengthen your resolve to act.

'Okay, alright then let's see how it goes,' offered Grace's husband, putting the kettle on, not at all convinced that her cunning plan would work, but willing to head up her support team.

Also, she figured that having some interests outside of work would give her a more balanced perspective and would expand her network, so when her wild waters time was calming she decided that, when she had recovered enough, she would think about supporting a first-time charity leader.

Helping someone else helps you, helps the other, builds a community. Win, win, win. Remember not to take on anything too demanding when you are in crisis.

Sarah (whose time is up, maybe)

Sarah had been meeting with her friends every first Wednesday of the month for ages. They enjoyed their favourite table by the window in their favourite café and put the world to rights with the help of tea and yummy cakes.

Alongside many fine offerings, a sign by the counter said 'The comeback is always stronger than the setback'. Everyone who visited the café knew what that meant.

As well as being in this fictional story, this quote sits proudly on the wall at the lovely and real Nutshells By-The-Sea café in Felixstowe, UK. It refers to the fire that had devastated the owners' previous café in Stowupland. The 'comeback' is indeed 'always stronger' if you do the personal and practical work to make it so, as the café owners did.

This same truth was also conveyed to me many years ago by a late friend and wise colleague on a day when, for me, it was all too much. I have found his advice to be true.

Recently, Sarah had been exploring the calming potential of camomile and was trying to put a brave face on the events of the day. 'Well it wasn't really working out. Alice was very sweet and well organized but, you know, she was rather young and she didn't really fit in with the way we do things.'

'Oh dear, so sorry to hear that, Sarah. How very trying for you.'

'You know Alice and her wife have somehow had a little one of their own who's just starting nursery,' said Sarah, 'and I'm not sure she was getting on with our families in quite the way I was expecting.'

Although sometimes out of touch with the life realities of those outside her circle, deep down Sarah, the founder, had a heart of gold. Indeed, with her husband's successful business, she could have bought herself a real one.

These were good friends and over the years they had each shared their stories of joy and sorrow, so they had heard a lot about Sarah's charity. They had helped her out now and again and had opened their fragrant gardens to raise much-needed funds.

On hearing of the departure of a third CEO in as many years they were concerned and critical in equal measure but didn't let on about the latter.

A gush of: 'Oh dear, not another one!' 'Really! I'm sorry to hear that.' 'You've put so much into it Sarah... How difficult for you.'

Then, as she squeezed a few drops of twisted lemon into her flavoured tea, her long-time friend looked Sarah in the eye and said, 'And what happened this time? Same as before?'

A CEO or Chair making one mistake once can be seen as good practice – failing faster can lead to succeeding quicker. But making the same mistake twice is carelessness. Making the same mistake three times tells you that you are missing something – there's a message shouting at you and you are just not getting it.

After an awkward pause the gush continued: 'What are you going to do... poor you, you must be exhausted.'

'Well yes, I couldn't get off last night actually. Took ages and then I had such a strange dream,' said Sarah awkwardly, as if she were still seeing the images of the night.

Although they were good friends, they didn't know whether to go there or not. Their conversation rarely got personal and had never gone off-piste into the events of the night. After a pregnant pause: 'How interesting. I think you can learn a lot from dreams. Don't you?'

Sarah saw this as an open invitation to dive back into the small hours of the night: 'You know, it was as if I'd been there before. I was in a dark room, there was a long line of people outside, and I knew they were all waiting for me. I didn't know why, I just knew they were all waiting and all wanted me, wanting something from me.'

Under the table and out of sight, Sarah's hands clasped tightly. 'It was so silly really, you know how dreams are. I just knew I had to get out of there. Next thing, I was outside somewhere, and I looked around and saw a sea of faces staring at me.'

Her lifelong best friend noticed Sarah's face reddening (and was that a bead of perspiration?).

'I just knew they were calling me, all of them. Then I was in a long gloomy corridor that had walls you could see through. I knew I could go through the walls and then suddenly I was out in the street. I knew I had to get away from them and had to get back to them too, but I couldn't find the way.'

Chattering from other tables in the café, a clatter of cutlery, the hiss of machines, cars passing, a siren in the distance – everyday sounds ran alongside Sarah's dream world.

'Then suddenly I was in a lift and pressed the "up" button. I had to get back and I knew that was going to take me back to them, but it didn't, it took down me to a big garden. I didn't know which way to go. Then I woke up in a panic. What a relief that was. How silly. What a nonsense.'

Sarah's best lifelong friend didn't think it was silly, nor did she think it was nonsense. Having just started a bereavement counselling course, she had become an instant expert in matters of life and death. 'Not silly Sarah, and not nonsense either, if you ask me,' she said sagely. Warming to her subject she added, 'To stay or not to stay, that is The Question.'

Sarah looked at her best friend, who looked rather pleased with herself having come up with such apposite wise words.

LISTEN TO GUT FEELINGS

This wasn't the first time Sarah had been confronted like this. Her husband, not one to mince his words ('I didn't get where I am today by beating about the bush'), had recently told her, 'You've already done more than enough. Time to go.' She worried and did nothing. But the firm voice of her husband kept coming back to her, hearing 'it's time to go... time to go... it's time...'

He went further and criticized her for not having any kind of exit interview, which, he firmly reminded her, is common practice in his world. How can you find out what went wrong and put it on record?

Earlier that day, when she had told him the dream, breakfast had been unusually tense. She had taken that tension with her as she set off for her monthly Wednesday meet.

For the first time, but not the last, she wondered whether one day she might think about 'The Question'.

A weak signal that keeps bleeping at you, triggered by a word overheard in the street or seen on a billboard, is telling you something that you have not wanted to hear. Don't ignore it. Amplify it. Listen to it. Respond.

Bob (is on the road to hell)

The buggers, Bob thought, *they hired me to turn this thing around and now I'm doing it they don't like it. I hit the ground running from the get-go, and it was all sweetness and light to start with. That Daniel is a wise guy. Been around a long time. Knows what's going on. Seems like the top guy's got my back, but I don't know about the rest of them.*

Neither the autumn sun pouring through the window nor the pulsing gym music were enough to drown out the grumbles inside Bob's head. Having had enough of pummelling the punch bag, he jumped onto the treadmill. Feet pounding, his thoughts racing, not in ordered sentences one after the other but like storm waves, furiously rising, turning, crashing around. Noise outside, noise inside. Like his job, he couldn't see beyond the treadmill.

Run. Faster. Harder.

As soon as I started to shake things up a bit and change the way we did things, it started going wrong. Maybe they didn't like my restructuring plans and persuading a few people to buck their ideas up. They said they wanted to bring things up to date, so why are they getting in my way? Why don't they just get over themselves so I can get on with it?

It had all started well enough but then there had been loads of little things in the last year that were crazy. Then a few months ago even weirder things started happening. Weird things that made no sense. Lengthy emails started flying around late into the evening, a few of the trustees never returned his calls, people didn't turn up when they had said they would and there were awkward moments at meetings.

Maybe they don't like my plans for restructuring, Bob thought.

Is the pace and volume of email chatter increasing, or getting less? Sit up and take notice of what's changing and in what way. If you see a rational explanation (e.g. a new project or big event coming up), breathe, keep calm and carry on. If you don't, it may mean that you are hearing the rumble of a waterfall up ahead.

The Head of Finance, who had been in post for over 20 years, didn't take kindly to being reminded that the accounts had to be done in a different way to follow new regulations (Bob had spent his teenage years being delinquent, but he was now spending his adult years diligently sticking to the rules).

Probably for too long, like the frog in slowly heating water, Bob had just put up with it. He was a tough guy and could cope with rough stuff. As it became ever more annoying, he just worked harder. Like now, thinking about it propelled him faster on the treadmill.

Tap the button, increase speed; nudge the lever, increase the gradient. Bob did both. Harder, harder, harder, faster, faster, faster. Head down, do it. I'll show them. With 'Road to Hell' blasting out on the gym's surround-sound system driving him on, his sweat dripped onto the spinning black belt.

Breathing hard, Bob pushed himself too far. Feeling a dizzying exhilaration and a sudden sharp jab in the chest, he grabbed the sides of the treadmill to stop himself. He knew he had hit his outer limit and was heading for a crash.

More by luck than judgement I lived through a hellish moment when I fell asleep and woke up a few long seconds later. Nothing so unusual about that – except that I was riding my 600cc motorbike at the time. Carrying major stress, I had slept no more than a few hours a night for many weeks, was a mile from home and couldn't keep my eyes open.

Every time I pass that junction I relive that moment and am deeply grateful for the wake-up call. That near-death experience prompted me to pluck up the courage to initiate a conversation the very next day with my boss (whom I didn't find to be an easy man, nor was it an easy conversation), which I should have faced months before. Straight after that conversation I negotiated an exit and then embarked on my career as an independent consultant, established get2thepoint, started my facilitation practice, coaching leaders in crisis, and also embarked on a long-postponed journey of inner exploration.

Glowing red and dripping wildly, Bob managed to slow the belt, and with gasping head down he pulled back from his moment of collapse. Just in time. He was on the edge.

'You okay?' said a passing personal trainer. Bob managed a 'yeah fine' as he staggered to the water cooler by the bench. 'You sure? Don't overdo it mate. I'm here if you need anything.' A spinning class instructor, he was smart, somewhat smarter than his T-shirt, which proclaimed 'The Beatings Will Continue Until Morale Improves'.

Yes, Bob was just about fine. He knew he had pushed himself to the limit. But that had been his way since he was a kid and so far he had got away with it.

We have learned ways to survive, to get through difficult times. These ways have been lifesavers – so far. But are they what you need now? Maybe this is a new situation you are facing and your old way of responding won't serve you now as it has done before. Doing the same old, same old may bring you to the same old point of collapse, and this time you might hit the wall. Let it go, think different.

Bob's work troubles had been expelled with every breath, making space for his inner voice, which murmured *spot those red flags* over and over, not too loudly but loud enough for Bob to hear.

He recalled that workshop at the conference a year ago – the one with the fire evacuation crowds spilling onto the street. *That was a crazy thing*, he thought, *how come no one smelled smoke, only me... or maybe they did but didn't do anything about it.* That had certainly been a warning that something was up, as indeed it was.

He remembered that, in the lunch queue, someone had wisely observed, 'You're not alone, we're all in it together, especially when you're in a tight corner.' *Like that Beatings Will Continue trainer,* thought Bob. *Good to know someone was watching out for me.*

Bob suddenly saw red. Not red of the angry kind but red of the waving flags kind. They had been waving wildly, but unseen. *I'm not going to put up with this crap. Got to do something. Got to sort it.*

Tough as he was, he felt nervous when he thought about his Chair, Daniel. *Yes, speak with him, he'll know what's up.* A determination grabbed him. *I'll speak with him this time next week at our Wednesday catch-up.*

Bob remembered what he had read somewhere, but couldn't quite place where, about how the hardest bit of having a courageous conversation is finding the courage to start – to move from permanently thinking about starting to actually dialling the number, writing an email or sending a text.

It was his turn with his son the coming weekend. 'He'd expect me to face up to it,' he told himself. 'Got to be a model for the young ones.'

'Let's face the music and dance.' *Endnote¹²*

Daniel the wise (is worried)

The other side of the street, through the windows of other city offices, Daniel saw a few keen souls at the end of their long days still straining at their screens, some with fingers tapping, others lost somewhere in email-land. An ordinary city day.

Out of his tenth-floor window, he could see a stream of bodies filling the pavement, most gazing at phones and thinking of somewhere else, not the present moment. A precious few were holding hands and chatting.

He practised healthy habits of doing the 'worst first' (get the task you don't like out of the way) and of getting his inbox to zero by the end of each day, but today he was much distracted by his chattering mind and by wondering what might be in the minds of others.

In principle get your inbox to zero at the end of each day. As part of your productivity system, get to know the relief of having processed quick (less than two minutes) tasks, deleting, delegating, organizing bigger tasks for later action and being able to start each new day with your inbox at zero. *Endnote*[13]

Seeing the bigger picture from his lofty vantage point, the stream became teeming ants whose squat little legs were carrying them home to their burrows (*Do ants have burrows?* he mused), content that they were now halfway through their working weeks.

The lives of others, he pondered. His late mother had sailed to England many decades ago to train as a midwife for the NHS. Although knowing little of what the family referred to as 'back home', the sense of service that his dear mother had brought with her lived in every cell of his body. Along with her diligence and tolerance, it had become part of Daniel's own way of being in the world and dealing with ever-present prejudices and troubles.

His end-of-day musing about his way up the greasy pole from the damp basement flat of his childhood to the C-suite was interrupted by a phone ringing, not his office landline, but his personal mobile.

The caller blasted, 'Hello Daniel, got a minute?' Daniel recognized the demanding voice of one of his fellow trustees, who always asked if he had a minute and then stole more. 'Look, this is getting a bit out of hand. It's not on, you know. I've just seen the draft for the annual meeting next month and he's put himself down to welcome our Honorary Patron. Surely that should be you, Daniel, or one of us, not the CEO. What's he up to?' Daniel couldn't get a word in.

I couldn't get a word in...

This wasn't the first punchy call he had been on the receiving end of over recent weeks. 'But that comes with the territory if you're a board Chair,' Daniel wisely said to himself. Mails and messages had been pouring down on him all week, not from everyone but from vocal long-standing trustees. He took a deep breath and exhaled long and slow, making sure not to reveal his weariness with the whole thing to the shrill caller.

Like two tunes playing at the same time, he heard the phone rant as a sort of descant, high above the bass notes of his own rumbling thoughts: *Why did I take this on? Maybe I shouldn't be standing for re-election when my term is up? Only another nine months to go.* Then, *Hold on, you're on the right track, keep going.*

'The others have been telling me they don't think it's right and you should do something. Who does he think he is? He's getting too big for his builder's boots. We've already extended his probation period haven't we, and everyone's saying we shouldn't be approving him in post.'

Daniel felt a tightening inside. 'Everyone.' He had heard this all too often. It's always 'the others', 'everyone', 'the whole board'; but he knew it was less than a handful banging their bin lids and whipping up a storm.

It happens. A private or third sector board, like any group, can fall into the old trap of creating and perpetuating a 'them and us' dynamic. 'Othering' drains energy and distracts. When differences of opinion emerge, there's a concomitant tendency to reinforce our own opinion, finding it easier to agree with those in our own bubble and trying to recruit others to join. This is dangerous in politics and it's dangerous on boards. Let's know our own mind, listen more and speak less.

Daniel thought of the simple wisdom of his dad, long since passed, who met each of his life struggles with a pithy aphorism, one for every situation on planet Earth. Both his parents had shared their wisdoms in little sound bites.

'To understand all is to forgive all' came to mind. Forgiveness might come later, but for now Daniel the wise was just trying to understand.

'Okay, yes, thank you, thank you for calling,' he said with an outer calm that belied his tightening shoulders, as if his body was telling him to fight and to hold back at the same time. 'I'll give it some thought and get back to you. Okay?' The caller said it was okay, but Daniel knew it wasn't really.

He wondered why they were raging about Bob. He had been by far the best candidate at interview last year; he was enthusiastic, knew how to get alongside the kids, and funders liked him too. Following the previous director, who had been a safe pair of hands and had done a solid job since the beginning, Bob was a breath of fresh air. He just needed to get his ego under control and to think before opening his mouth. Bob was a smooth talker, which some found beguiling, others found annoying.

His coat on to protect him against the autumn evening chill, Daniel headed round the corner to meet a Chair of substantial experience who, happily, was also an experienced coach. Very timely. Daniel needed help. Arranged by an association for nonprofit chairs, they had met several times already and Daniel knew he was a good listener. *Endnote*[4]

'Good to see you. I've got a bit of a thing going on. I need some good ideas about what to do next. I need to get my head clear because all about me are losing theirs, you know what I mean?'

'Yes I do,' said listener Chair, who had recently recovered from his own wild waters times. 'Go ahead.'

After two hours in which Daniel had aired his heart and soul, he emerged feeling greatly relieved and knew what he needed to do. Although this was set up as a mutual support arrangement, he was impressed with how today the listener parked his own stuff and had listened; he had listened well. After saying nothing for a long while, the listener had asked one clarifying question and then a second incisive question that touched the core of what was happening. This question unlocked Daniel's thinking about what he needed to do next.

I see my coaching sessions as a hunt for treasure. It's there, waiting to be found.

The person to whom I am listening is full of their story. With patience I listen. I know there will be tangents, non sequiturs, foggy moments, emotions, perhaps some silences.

When times are calm and the water is still you can see clearly through it. But when it's turbulent you can't see through to the bottom. There's so much rushing noise from the raging waters that it's difficult to distinguish between flotsam floating past and a gem. So I listen more.

Then comes a moment when something my client says stands out, sparkles or has weight, something that attracts my attention. It may be related to the very first thing that was said in an unguarded moment at the beginning of the session.

Maybe we have found a nugget of treasure. I will sit with it to see if it continues to stand out, sparkle, have weight and attract my attention. If it starts to feel more and more solid I offer it. 'I hear you say…'

If I'm feeling more sure about it, I will offer it with more emphasis; if I'm less sure, I will offer it tentatively: 'Could it be that…' 'I wonder if…' 'Am I hearing something about…' 'Do you think there might be…'

Then I wait to see how it's received. Did it strike a chord? It may be the treasure that unlocks new thinking, which can open up a next action.

On his way home, without thinking, Daniel opened up his email. Bad idea. Among the junk trivia inviting him to buy, listen to and join things in which he had no interest, were emails from fellow trustees, each one longer than the last and variously expressing support for and criticism of their CEO. Many had shouty subject lines, some were in CAPITALS. 'That's messed up my evening,' he grumbled.

You have 24 hours in a day, no choice. But you can choose how you use your attention. Use this most precious resource to focus on the stuff that will help you get to where you need to get to. Simple in principle, hard in practice. Try, fail, keep trying.

Rose (into the flames)

Vivid images, clear characters and colours too. Rose had withdrawn into a weird world like a turtle in some faraway place pulling its little legs 'indoors' to protect itself. That world was one she knew well, only too well.

There was a startled-looking figure with a distant expression, as if it was only half there. The figure was singing and swaying awkwardly with floating arms. Fading in and out, the figure was wearing chunky look-at-me headphones. No words. With a pale complexion the figure had sleek grey hair with pink streaks.

Half in, half out, hanging between her real dream and her real living room worlds, a bead of sweat dripped onto the crimson cushion.

As the living room world won the struggle between her inner and outer worlds, a shiver overtook Rose as she remembered her regular monthly meeting with the Chair a while back, when he had mentioned casually that a couple of the new trustees were going on about mergers with other arts charities. 'Nothing to worry about,' he had said.

So she hadn't worried about it and just got on with the job. Until that Friday at 4pm precisely.

That afternoon was the moment her world had flipped, and she had been plunged into raging wild waters. They handed her a letter giving notice of redundancy. 'You can't do that, I set up the charity. I'm running everything, you can't make me redundant,' she said. But they did anyway and told her that she must not contact any staff, even though there was a new member of staff who was in the middle of a funding bid to the Lottery and was soon to present at a conference.

She went into a spin, didn't know what was up and what was down, and since that day the week before last had been in a state of high anxiety that was giving her a near permanent headache.

'They stole my "I can" from right under my nose,' she complained to her good friend, a headteacher who was busy trying to keep her head above water.

After a couple of weeks of no sleep and preferring alternative remedies to conventional medicine, that afternoon she had visited a healer offering aromatherapy massage and strong Chinese medicinal herbs. 'They'll help you relax,' said the healer.

Indeed, she was so relaxed when she got home that she dropped into a deep sleep in her favourite chair in front of her favourite arts programme, which she watched every Wednesday evening. And as that deep sleep overcame her, she had been transported to the weird dream world with singing and floating arms.

Hanging unhappily between dream and living room she thought of those long-gone glory days of community arts while her dream-world singer sang '… the times… they are a-chang… ing'.

Impermanence is a central truth of Buddhism and is an objectively verifiable fact. What is now, will change: 'the times', my life, the way things are, humanity, planet Earth and beyond, will always change. With impermanence comes hope.

In her daylight confusion Rose knew it *was* all changing and always had been, was getting faster and she couldn't keep up anymore. Not only that, but at her age she didn't really want to.

… running things for 24 years… running for 24 years… for 24 years…

Then, *I've done enough.*

She heard an inner voice murmuring through her sleepy haze, '… redundancy… not a proper redundancy', and more words '… gardening leave… did you see that coming?… go on, fight them, hang in there, don't throw it all away'.

To be legal, a redundancy in the UK must meet certain criteria, such as the organization no longer being a going concern or changing the nature of its work so needing a new skill set.

Half waking, half in dark daylight dream, Rose remembered the excitement of those heady days, her first real-love relationship and now being on her own. But with the scraps of her dream still with her, she felt some kind of community connection going on. *Good to know I'm not the only one.*

Suffering is a fact of life, and if you know how to suffer, you will suffer less.

After some while and with the unreal dream voices still playing in her mind for real, Rose landed back on her real armchair. She now heard just two voices, both her own. One told her, *Fight it. Go on, stand up to them*, the other, *Let go, you've done enough.* The voices pulled her one way and the other and each was equally compelling.

In her drowsiness she couldn't stop her circular repetitive thinking: the board had got excited about the possibility of more mergers with other inner-city arts projects, as the last one had gone so well. They had hired a consultant, who had worked with one of the board members to come up with some proposals. It had been made clear that the board would take the lead.

Although organizational structure is a proper matter of interest to the trustees as it affects the longer term of the organization, it's also a proper matter for a CEO to be closely involved with. CEO, team, Chair, trustees – all have their part to play in discussions about structure. This is not something to be left to board or executive team alone.

Why didn't I try to stop them? I should've done. I couldn't have, they wouldn't listen. But if you had, it would be different now. It's all my fault...

Awake now, Rose started to write all the reasons why and why not she should fight to stay, and all the reasons why and why not she should let go and leave. Pages, pages and more pages of valuable scribble. She had found this writing-to-get-your-mind-clear exercise helpful other times when she had been stuck. And she found it so this time. *Handy*, she thought, *for my first conversation with that coach guy tomorrow. Got to get things sorted.*

You are going under; confused and in desperation, you reach out for help. You find that a hand, grounded enough to withstand the drag of the most violent undercurrents, is there to hold you, keeping your head above water and guiding you until, eventually, one day the waters will calm.

One day yes, but not today. Because today is the day of my first coaching conversation with a new client, which may go something like this:

'I don't know where to start.'

'That's okay, just start anywhere.'

At last, someone is listening. With relief, the floodgates open. Then comes a rush of facts, fears and muddle as the story is told, not in neat chronological order, nor in order of what's most significant, but in a tumble jumble of whatever comes to mind. The drama unfolds.

An outpouring of pent-up distress takes time. A couple of hours is not unusual, and I make that time available, or if I don't have the time I just introduce myself and arrange a time when I do.

'... take your time, it's okay. We have a good couple of hours now and can fix another time soon if we need to...' There's no rush to find a solution. This first contact establishes trust.

I listen until enough of the story is told, for now. There's relief. There may be tears upon hearing that there's enough space now and that I will be there 'until the end of the chapter' – as long as the crisis goes on, which may be weeks, months, a year of more. Their pace is my pace, within my diary constraints.

Within that mutually understood frame, it's a gift of compassionate listening and 'unconditional positive regard' centred on the person, until the crisis is over.

Sometimes I wait as the speaker goes further; sometimes I notice or invite them to go deeper. Further... deeper...

I don't bring clever tips and coaching tricks, but simply bring myself in the moment. My being present means that I feel the person I'm with at the same time as being in touch with my own inner response.

This 'therapeutic use of self' means that my self is my primary tool. With self as instrument, I draw on my personal characteristics and, within parameters, am personally available to the person I'm with, in service to their path ahead. *Endnote¹⁵*

The valuable scribbled pages together with notes of the coaching session lay scattered over the living room table for a week.

Rose looked at them every day and, as she did so, her resolve strengthened, until a couple of Wednesdays later, with the company of her favourite TV arts programme, she lit a fire in the grate and committed the pages one by one into the flames. Rose knew the power of ritual. *It's time to go; 24 years is enough. There's loads of other things I want to do. Time to move on.*

I'm reminded of a powerful ritual in a summer retreat when many hundreds of us went through a process of reflection that ended with writing what we each wanted to let go of, and then all of us as so moved, one at a time placed our papers in the campfire.

I have also let go of a burden by letting a handwritten note float and sink to the bottom of a local pond; when I went there the next day it had disappeared without trace. What a relief to see it gone.

Alice (meets the ghost of interviews past)

It all seemed so obvious now Alice was looking back on it.

'Why didn't I think?'

'Yes, why didn't you?'

'The way they were talking, you know, it just didn't feel right.'

'I told you, didn't I, but you didn't listen.'

Walking hand in hand that chilly autumn day, their little one having a happy time with Grandma, this was their regular Wednesday afternoon walk. A friend had suggested that Alice should practise self-compassion and her wife was content to have a break from her home office. As on all recent Wednesdays, their main topic of conversation was That Job.

They had spoken about That Job a lot over the last year. Alice was still struggling to make it work, which it still wasn't, and she wondered how much longer she could hang on. Her partner was doing her best to be understanding but had heard it all before and was getting weary of it.

Crunching their way through the early autumn leaves, they walked by the same park bench on which Alice had rehearsed for her interview. She remembered those days and her excitement at getting That Job as if it had happened yesterday. But it wasn't yesterday; she'd had the interview a year ago.

'Why didn't you see what was staring you in the face?'

The Ghost of Interviews Past and Alice's wife were speaking with one voice. 'You didn't do your due diligence, did you? You just raced ahead all excited. You were so keen on getting a job, you didn't think. Not smart, not smart at all!' Alice got the message now, but she hadn't heard it a year ago. She saw more clearly now.

She remembered that founder Chair Sarah, who appeared poorly prepared, had asked Alice why she used personal pronouns, had done most of the talking and had made vague promises about moving offices, meanwhile offering no clarity about finance.

The sun was setting at the close of this chilly day and the clouds on the horizon were delivering a spectacular sunset. Alice saw the wispy clouds, which had taken on the shape of flags in the sky. 'Nice when clouds look like things,' she said. Endnote¹⁶

They were tinged with a reddening evening glow, not unlike the red flags that had been waving a year ago in the interview. There had been more than enough red flags to raise the alarm; Alice judged herself for having missed them all.

Alice was a robust character, and happily her wife's income was secure, at least for now. So after a year of trying as best she could and having a tough time of it, she had begun to think the unthinkable, to leave.

'But I'd feel such a failure,' Alice had said earlier. 'This is my first CEO job.'

'Maybe it'll all be for the best dear,' Grandma had replied.

'Want bizgit,' their daughter had said.

'Just do it,' said her partner briskly.

Don't give up, was Alice's mantra. She had always been a trier. So she kept on trying.

Imran (is hit in the guts, twice)

Imran was hitting the phones. Hitting the keyboard. And he had flashes of hitting his boss too, who at that moment was some thousands of miles away at a very important meeting in New York.

Today, Wednesday, it was now five hectic days since he had been summoned to his boss's office at the end of last week. No warning and, as it turned out, no job either.

'Sorry, Imran, as you know, the company has been urgently reviewing its operations and I have to tell you that we've been told to downsize. I'm sorry to have to tell you that your position has to go. I did the best I could but… well, you know how things are.'

Shock happens. I know. I came home from my 50th birthday trip to southern Africa (the one with the wild water adventure) to find a brutal lawyer's letter on the doormat...

'I see you've been with us for just under two years. HR will be in touch.'

This was a body blow of failure. 'I can't tell Dad, and Mum won't know what to say to her friends,' Imran said to himself, feeling shame.

Until that moment he'd had an eye on the higher echelons of the company, but Imran – now having heard the company was reviewing their operations – was reviewing his too. His time with the company had all started so well, but had got rocky recently since the new US owners arrived.

He had never really been in love with investment banking (*Is anyone?* he wondered) but now the shine had definitely rubbed off. 'There's more to life than this,' said his good friend over a drink, and Imran agreed.

Firing off emails and messages to all his contacts, his fury became his fuel. Imran was going full steam ahead into his future. He was well thought of and his web of contacts were responding quickly with a mix of messages of resigned condolence ('It happens' 'You'll be alright'), fellow feeling and the odd pointer ('How about... have you thought of... maybe the old firm has got something?').

Among the flow of mostly helpful responses, one stood out, not because it was eloquently phrased, in capitals or yellow highlight, but because it hit Imran in the gut. He clicked the link and the ad jumped off the page. It made no sense – no money, a different type of organization altogether, although still working with numbers, which was his thing.

His close friend, who was good and wise with it, encouraged him. 'They'll love you. Charities are looking for people like you, with solid financial experience. Follow that up and you'll get a paid job too, you'll see. It will open new doors.'

'Go for it... you won't regret it,' said his friend. Imran did go for it. He knew about investing in his future... and a year later he wasn't regretting it for one minute.

A tumble of worries

These nine characters are each navigating their wild Wednesdays. Meanwhile, other good leaders are too. Many miles apart and each feeling alone, good leaders everywhere are trying to survive wild waters.

In their own traumas, they forget the truth that they are not the only good leaders going through turbulent times. While many good leaders may be groaning alone, they could be sharing together.

Our struggles are eased when we share as part of a community of fellow travellers, especially if those fellow travellers are working for a better world.

I am part of half a dozen online communities, meeting weekly, monthly or quarterly. I find that listening quietly and speaking from the heart is enriching and enlightening and helps me clarify my thinking. In spiritual circles this may be called a 'sangha', and for me they are my islands of sanity and safety.

'I'll never work again. My reputation is shot to bits. I don't know what to do. It's all over. How am I going to explain all this to anyone who might want to employ me? They'll find out what's been going on and I'll never get a reference and everyone will know I'm a failure. I need to earn, and anyway I like working and...'

Even if a bit tarnished for a short while, your reputation won't be trashed. If things have gone wrong, you will never really know what people are saying about it behind your back. But remember that they see what has happened in the context of knowing that bad stuff often happens and also what they know of you from direct experience. Also, their main preoccupation will be with what's going on for them, not with you. Get over it. Even if it is dented a bit, your reputation will bounce back.

I was afraid of my reputation being damaged during my wild waters times. My good friend (who happened to be Head of HR in a big charity at the time) told me it would be okay, and it was.

'I'm tired all the time.'

'My daughter has just started school and saw me crying. She's finding it hard, and I can't be there for her like I want to be.'

'I try not to watch the news. It's horrible seeing all those wars and everything messed up. It stirs me up so much.'

'It shouldn't be this warm at this time of year. It's autumn. The climate is changing. It's getting worse.'

'Those AI bots are going to take over. And what's the "G" in AGI anyway?'

'Radical hope' is a vision of new possibilities in the face of personal or collective devastation. A catalytic ingredient at the heart of personal transformations, it can help us rise from the ashes of collapse and step into a better yet unknown future. *Endnote*[7]

'Money's getting short. Looks like my partner's going to be made redundant, so I'll be the main breadwinner. We've been in the flat for a couple of years and have got a big mortgage, but I guess, if it came to it, we'd have to go and live with her mum, but I really don't fancy that for an idea. I could always go back to teaching if I had to, that'd pay the bills, but that's yesterday's stuff.'

'I've always been pretty fit, but I've had a check-up at hospital and they sent a letter saying they need to see me again to check a growth.

They say it's probably benign – "nothing to worry about but best to check". That's playing on my mind and the check-up appointment has just been postponed again.'

'My best friend has just found a lump. Cancer. We've known each other for years. No, no, no, please not.'

'My friend's son has just told him that they're non-binary. I want to understand but I don't get it.'

'Our lovely pet dog just died. You can't rehearse grief.'

'Noisy neighbours, I can't relax'.

'Menopause. I'm finding it hard to cope.'

'It's getting hard at home. Tensions from work are spilling out over the kitchen table. We had a flaming row the other day. My partner is so angry with them, he wants to go down there and sort them out. He's telling me just to chuck it in. But I can't, I don't want to give up and I'm not going to give in either. I'm going to leave when I decide, not when someone else does.'

'The boiler's just broken down and the guy said we need a new one. We can't afford that, no way. The nights are drawing in.'

'My dad's just been diagnosed with Alzheimer's. He needs looking after. It's been getting worse and now he's getting aggressive. Mum's at her wit's end and it's a three-hour round trip to their place. The radiator's leaking, the car's rattling and I've lost my bank card. All on top of what's happening at work.'

Whatever may happen to us, no one can take from us the choice of how we respond.

This is our Wild Waters time.

This is your very own PhD in leadership. Crisis provokes insight under pressure. It's hard, hard, hard, but in that chaos hold the belief that one day you will look back, know that you survived and see this was as powerful a time of learning as it was painful.

Since 2002 I have been engaged by ACEVO as an associate to support charity CEO members who feel they are in a crisis/that their job is under threat. This is part of their wider support team.

Contact with the client doesn't follow a predetermined pattern (e.g. every Tuesday, 50 minutes for six sessions) but is arranged as and when needed. A crisis, like a river, does not flow predictably and smoothly from beginning to end and, especially when flowing fast, is full of unexpected turbulence. There may be sudden storms. To make it safely down the river calls for an acute sense of what's happening right now and the agility to respond as needed.

I communicate by phone (occasionally video), in-person meetings, being a professional friend at hearings, offering comment on sensitive emails. Whatever is needed. The benefit of short messages far outweighs the few moments they take to write. 'How are things?' 'Good luck today with the meeting/ return to work...' 'Thinking of you, how are you doing?'

Chapter 3
FEET BACK ON DRY LAND, ANOTHER YEAR LATER

COPE, HEAL, RECOVER

One year and a day after their wild Wednesdays,
everyone has survived their crisis and are up a mountain,
appearing on TV, enjoying lucky meetings…

Robin (dreams up a gum tree)

To get through those difficult days of a year ago, Robin had persuaded himself into the habit of starting his day with a morning walk. He often woke up with a tangled head, and the bite of early morning fresh air cleared away the cobwebs. His morning walk had become his essential time to think, to settle his turbulent mind and to ponder the meaning of things.

The more he saw the trees, the more he came to see them as his steady forever friends, stretching back over time, solid, stable, forever.

We see the tree's bark, branches, leaves. We know that there are tree elements that we do not see, such as roots, sap and age rings. And there's more we do not see. Think of that tree as a seed and the tree that seed came from; we may also pause to ponder the countless generations of trees and people that have gone before, right back to the very first. (If that's too hard to think of, try the last seven generations.)

Perceiving beyond what we see before our eyes may help us put today's struggles in context.

On his very long gardening leave, Robin had been pulled back from the edge by the chance kindness of an early morning dogwalker by a canal who would never know the saving power of his few generous words of greeting.

During five turbulent months the investigation had been set up, interviews undertaken, report written, circulated, amended, circulated again and presented to a closed meeting of trustees who were getting thoroughly fed up with the whole thing. Two trustees had resigned, citing work pressures, key staff had left, the charity (and Robin) had spent lots of money on lawyers and, meanwhile, an interim CEO had made valiant efforts to keep the ship afloat.

As the case was not strong and as the working relationship was irreparably damaged, lawyers had advised a settlement agreement. The board had blinked first and had suggested a 'without prejudice' conversation.[13]

Soon thereafter Robin walked away with some cash, a stash of unexpressed anger, a wounded ego and a burning sense of guilt and failure. He knew his wife had been on the edge of seeking divorce.

---

[13] 'Without prejudice' means that statements that are made (in a genuine attempt to settle a dispute) cannot subsequently be used in formal proceedings as evidence of admissions against the party that made them. This frees parties to engage in conversations to seek a mutually agreeable solution.

Some, by no means all, of the CEOs I have coached through crisis have come to a settlement agreement and left. It may be the best option available, but is not a brilliant outcome. As well as a financial settlement and agreed public statement about the reason for leaving and reference, it drains energy and leaves a bad taste that lingers. Best to see the wild waters coming and take evasive action. Even if relationships are damaged beyond repair, consider playing your part in finding a mutually respectful resolution that minimizes damage to all parties.

Now walking by a stream on a bright morning Robin recalled the cold dark moment a year earlier by the edge of that canal when he first started realizing his deep need for nature as well as his need to get the trauma out of his system. His venture into nature coaching served both needs.

Today was special as it was the first Thursday of the month and today was his sixth session walking in nature with his coach. After monthly in-person sessions, his coach was now trying online sessions and Robin was pleased with the freedom of having her tucked away on his phone, walking alongside him.

You have to walk with your own pain, but you do not have to walk alone.

Being in nature with a coach as guide, together drawing on nature's wisdom and nourishment, was a powerful combination. Robin found that there was something about having a natural landscape all around him that helped him to reconnect with what was going on in his inner landscape. It helped him see things in perspective, the brisk autumn weather helping him connect with his inner weather. Robin loved it.[14]

He walked, he talked, she listened. Sitting on a conveniently placed log he sipped his decaff from his reusable flask. Today, like in each session, he went on a journey over the years, recalling the high spots and the lows. He heard the trees, he saw the squirrels scampering, the ducks variously paddling and squabbling, he smelled the warming damp earth. Nourishing nature and his coach had gently conspired to get his feet back on the ground and to help him recognize the pain, accept his part in creating it and to begin to heal.

I see my relationship with the person I'm coaching as a long walk together. They must walk their path, as we all do, and I'm alongside them. I walk close and a bit behind, so they can easily turn to me as needed. They know I'm there and may hold me in mind when we are not in direct contact. From my own coaching relationship with Nancy Kline over 14 years up to 2016 I know how enriching this kind of walking together relationship can be.

---

[14] Lesley Roberts *Coaching Outdoors: The Essential Guide to Partnering with Nature in Your Coaching Conversations* (2023).

Seeing the clear blue sky framing golden autumn leaves, this was Robin's time to rest. His session over, the soft moss invited him to lie down and digest.

Having space is an essential prerequisite of healing. A wounded animal knows this and we do too, but are driven by our habits and forget. We may find that space in nature, music, the attention of a friend or professional guide, meditation – any time we free ourselves to turn our attention inwards for a few moments.

Robin's rest drifted into sleep, and in his dreams he heard voices from leaders who, once upon a time, had crossed his path.

THE POWER
OF
PAUSES

These are the kind of things I have heard from leaders I have coached, albeit not all at once as presented here but over many years.

'You did what!!?'

'Well it was a staff party, everyone was feeling quite jolly. So we had a little kiss in the corner... but only once.'

'But he was your head of finance, right? Not a good idea, my friend. Not a good idea at all.'

'Hmm yes. From that day our working relationship went off the rails.'

'Everyone was gossiping about that kiss and giggling. Tittle-tattle tales echoed everywhere. Silly thing to do. But it seemed like a good idea at the time.'

Robin dosed, a breeze brushed the leaves and more dream voices came and went.

'That's the worst, isn't it?'

'It was horrible. It was his everyday bullying that added up. Little things like nasty offhand comments in front of other people and sending Friday night emails about small things in BIG CAPITALS, demanding an answer the next morning.'

'God, it gets worse!'

'Like in private telling me the report was all good, then trashing it in public at the board meeting a week later.'

'Ouch! Embarrassing.'

'It hit me hard. More than embarrassing. A nightmare. Dissing me, he was.'

With Robin's steady breathing, his dream voices tumbled over one another.

'What? No appraisal!?'

'What? She changed the minutes of the meeting!?'

'What? The Chair was there for 30 years? And wouldn't go! Not on.'

'What? No up-to-date policies for anything?'

More dreamy voices were bubbling up but were drowned out by a rumble of thunder. Pulse suddenly racing and eyes now wide open, Robin awoke to see dark clouds gathering. But unlike two years before, he saw the storm coming and took evasive action.

Heading home, his pulse returning to normal, he recalled the voices of his vivid dream and mused, *Do any of that stuff and you're definitely up a gum tree.*

Grace (carries the spirit of Saint Bernard)

Grace was now sleeping better. She had slept right through that night, waking only once briefly to the wind rattling the windows. After the turbulent times of the last couple of years, at last she was finding some rest on this Thursday.

After 25 years, her Chair had eventually done the right thing and had resigned, and this had opened the way for a board member to step up, declaring it would be for 'just a few months' while a new incumbent was found.

Terms of office should be formally agreed that typically are a maximum of three (three-year) terms. Not having a policy about terms of office inevitably means it gets personal when eventually it's time for a trustee, even more so for a Chair, to go; there's trouble ahead.

As she surfaced from her refreshing slumber Grace thought back to those 'just a few months', which became six then 12. Grace had to work hard at her relationship with her trustee acting as Vice-Chair and Chair, who constantly meddled in operational details.

For a while she had managed to tolerate it, but when he overruled her decision to reimburse volunteer expenses of just £50, she decided it was time to act. That kind of operational decision as stated in the scheme of delegation, agreed long ago, was for her to make as CEO. Now she was going to stand up for what was right. *That's what I'm paid for isn't it?*

Choosing to see this not as a principle but as a personality conflict, other board members had said the two of them should go to mediation. It took months to arrange, with each side proposing their own trusted person to mediate; and when the meeting finally did happen with a mediator whom neither party felt totally comfortable with, it failed. Of course it did. Neither party felt safe enough to engage and each had said their piece and, despite the best efforts of the mediator, listened with closed ears and hearts.

Having been set up as a small project by a local church many decades ago, the organization was grounded in a deep religious ethos, and now there was a disagreement, everyone claimed that God was on their side. Eventually, as neither prayer nor mediation had worked, they employed a firm of lawyers.

'Amazing that I can conjure up those characters,' Grace mused as she poured her morning cuppa. This had been a repeating night and daydream for a while, always with some warming imagery, often an open fire, sometimes featuring cups of tea with warm words in the air. She knew they were not from nowhere but from inside. She knew all these characters were hers, all creatures of her unconscious working 24/7 to make sense of the world.

A big friendly dog was a regular reverie visitor. *That's odd*, she thought. *Which bit of me is that big caring dog that kept coming over to me and putting its head on my lap?* It was like one of those giant Saint Bernards that do alpine rescues. Although not a great lover of dogs, to Grace this one seemed to embody care, affection and duty, while also being strong, skilful and determined. Grace carried her very own saintly 'Saint B' inside her.

To Grace, Saint B seemed to carry the hope of a better world. She knew that while she carried the image of that big caring dog with her, there would be hope; Saint B was like a mix of all the best people she had ever met in civil society since her first job in an inner-city youth project set up by her church.

Those days were tough. She remembered the softly spoken supervisor in her very first youth job, who somehow managed to be open and closed, friendly and firm all at the same time. He was able to shut out the crazy druggy stuff going on around him and the kids liked him even when he disciplined them. She carried his memory with her too.

We know we and others will mess up. It happens. So we continually need to restart, to 'begin anew', a practice in which we appreciate the qualities of another person, express regret at what we have done, share our hurt feeling and ask for their support for the future. *Endnote*[18]

Often in her night and daydreams, Saint B wandered to each person in turn, variously nuzzling with its nose and putting its large warm head in someone's lap, or just standing there and, well, looking caring and charitable. Saint B was an embodiment of the best of civil society spirit.

In what may be called our 'store consciousness', we each carry wholesome 'seeds' such as tolerance, understanding, non-violence, joy, and more; we also carry seeds of jealousy, hatred, anger, fear and despair. In turbulent times, if we choose to work for a better world, we may also choose to nourish the wholesome 'seeds' and leave the unwholesome seeds to rest unwatered. Thereby we nourish the decency and love in us and are the civil society we long to see.

This is a dose of just what the doctor ordered, thought Grace, ready for the new day. *I'll be back to work from next Monday, so I'll get some fresh air today.*

The lawyer's investigation, commissioned by the board, had found that there was indeed substance to Grace's grievance about the Vice-Chair-now-Chair's, behaviour. Nothing criminal, nothing immoral, but quite a lot that was poor practice and had been undermining Grace and the charity's mission.

Now it was the Vice-Chair-now-Chair's chance to do the proper thing, and he did. Having thought about it for longer than was strictly necessary after the lawyer's report landed, not only did he resign but two of her close allies on the board also resigned, one citing work pressures, the other grandchildren duties.

Yes, a walk will be good for me. Need to get my mojo back. After two months of sick leave while the lawyers did their work, the way was now clear for Grace to go back to work. Shoes on, waterproof in her backpack, off she went to walk through the park to her favourite café. There was a growing sense of hope in the air. As she took her first step outside, she saw cumulus clouds passing away to the horizon, no longer rattling her and the windows. The air was fresh with the smell of fallen leaves.

She carried the spirit of Saint B along with her too, ready to be called to mind at will.

Grace saw a child playing, an elderly couple walking and talking, a runner full of gritty determination to achieve a personal best. A dog trotted past. An oak tree stood solid and stable, as was its nature. The swaying branches of a distant willow, which knew how to bend with the breeze, touched the stream.

She had probably passed by all these things before but hadn't noticed them through the fog of her distress. *That's okay*, she thought, *I see them now*. Life had always been good and now she was able to see it that way. She smiled at the nature of things. She hadn't seen them before but now she noticed the civil qualities of determination, strength, generosity and flexibility living all around her.

Suddenly…

'Django, come back. Django! *Django!!*' Grace's reverie was sharply interrupted as Django raced ever further away from his master, making a beeline for a huddle of ducks at the edge of the park pond. Dogs do that kind of thing. As Django closed in on them, the ducks fluttered away wearily (although it was still early, for the third time today), leaving their pursuer looking perplexed and triumphant in equal measure.

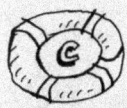

You can choose R&R or R&R.

You can:

React and Retaliate

or

Reflect and Respond

Get it?

Only as his basic instinct loosened its iron grip, did Django hear and heed his master's voice. He looked round and trotted back to his owner. Job done. He didn't spare a passing thought about the possibility that if there had been a busy road between him and the ducks he might have been chasing ducks in doggy heaven.

The reptilian brain is the oldest of the three parts of the brain and controls the body's vital functions. It includes the main structures found in a reptile's brain, namely the brainstem and the cerebellum. It shouts loudly when our basic instincts are provoked by the immediate prospect of satisfying our primal needs or when we fear they are threatened.

When our position as a leader is challenged, our reptilian brain is flooded with fears about status, money, confidence, adequacy. The higher-functioning part of our brain is overwhelmed and ignored, and we may be propelled into misjudged and pointless pursuits.

Fight, flight, fawn, freeze. We are bombarded by a cacophony of competing voices driving us to fight or flight, or we may find ourselves trying to win favour by fawning (servile flattery). Having no idea which way to go, we may freeze (think rabbit in headlights).

The café at the edge of the park had become a haven, a sanctuary even, for Grace during the most challenging times. It was a place to hear the birds, plant her feet firmly on the ground and to reconnect with normal life; she found reassurance in the hum of conversation among clattering cups and everyday chatter. '… we'll get that sorted then... did she really say that!... got to go, meeting at two... have you seen the stuff in the sale next door...?' All reassuringly familiar.

I saw a grey-haired woman in a local café gazing pensively towards the river. I had seen her several times before, always lost in thought. One day we spoke. She said, 'I lost my husband a few years ago. I was in a desperate state, thinking dark thoughts.'

She told me she had chanced upon this café, this seat, this view and that it was 'my sanctuary'. It's still her safe place. I confided in her that sanctuary, a quiet place with little or no external stimuli, was becoming ever more important for me too.

Although the early morning rush had all but subsided, the place was full and humming with a warm Thursday, nearly the end-of-the-week feel to it. The silent TV in the corner conveniently offered subtitles for anyone who thought of looking up.

As she headed for an empty seat by the window, Grace felt an impulse: *Look over there, over there.* Out of the corner of her eye she saw a just-cleaned table with two empty armchairs looking invitingly familiar. 'Another Chair, another Chair...' had a distant familiar ring to it. The chairs had her name on them and a few moments later her backside had landed on one of them too, with her heart and soul arriving just a few moments later. She found herself humming one of her favourite songs, 'Let Your Soul Be Your Pilot'.[15]

---

[15] 'Let Your Soul Be Your Pilot', Sting. Released on Mercury Falling 1996, inspired by a friend who was suffering from AIDS.

I'll let the queue go down a bit. I've done enough rushing about, now I need to recover and get ready to go back to work to lead the clear up. Yes, she had stood up for what she believed was right and had been suspended and then was on sick leave. The investigation dragged on and meanwhile the management team had soldiered on in her absence. Distracted and without leadership they had let many important deadlines slip but nevertheless had just about survived. They were all battered and bruised, as was Grace.

Resting her weary bones, Grace saw the everyday café trivia of jumbled heaps of cups, wrappers and cutlery, which reminded her of chaotic images she had seen all too often on the news. She thought of work. One heap of rubble had 'creaking organizational systems' written all over it, others 'strained relationships', 'delayed funding applications', and another 'damaged reputation'. There were more. Grace saw rubble everywhere and chose not to blame but to focus her attention on what she would do next.

The *Trümmerfrauen* (rubble women) helped clear bombed cities in Germany and Austria after the Second World War, when 3.6 million of the 16 million homes in German cities were destroyed and even more were damaged. Over a third of all infrastructure, school buildings, factories were damaged or destroyed. After a war, and indeed after any time of organizational crisis, there's some clearing up to do. Endnote[19]

Although she knew that what she was facing was on a far smaller scale than that faced by those rebuilding war-torn cities, she also saw that its root cause – human folly and the failure of governance – was the same. Invoking the spirit of Saint B, she pondered the fragility of the human condition, but she found the spirit in her not to blame. She generously saw that the Vice-Chair acting as Chair had behaved in good faith, albeit with somewhat too much faith and too little common sense.

Good governance enhances life, poor governance depletes, damages and may destroy.

The flood of customers was dwindling, and Grace waited, inviting good fortune to come her way.

Alice (follows a whisper)

A little while after her brief acquaintance with what's referred to by some as founder syndrome, Alice was well on the road to recovery. She had done her very best, but after a year or so she was unceremoniously informed by the founder Chair that her very best was actually not good enough. 'Sorry,' said Sarah darkly, 'people are not happy,' but she stopped short of saying which people and what they were not happy about. Being told to go without adequate explanation was a blow but, having been on the edge of handing in her notice anyway, Alice felt a sense of relief.

With much less than the length of service needed to have protected employment rights, she had left with nothing other than extra pages in her book of experience and the still quite new coffee swooshing machine that the team had decided would be a fitting farewell gift.

After some while of having more time at home with her toddler than she had planned, and with the help of her mentor, Alice had taken herself in hand and resolved to do everything she needed to do to get over her rocky experience. Yes, she had youth on her side, but also a toddler at her feet, and money wasn't overflowing.

That's life, she thought philosophically. *Move on*.

Recovering from any physical or emotional trauma will take time and attention, but it can be done. We may survive the trauma by freezing, an intelligent reaction at the time. It is possible to unfreeze, rediscover energy and at the same time become a remedy for others. *Endnote*[20]

Alice couldn't afford the gym, so she walked. She couldn't easily afford to go out with her friends, so they got together in each others' living rooms. Her friends said Alice was 'on-it'. Never a big meat eater, she now stopped altogether; 'Cheaper and healthier,' she said. She decided to do something new, so she joined her local wild water swimming group (which reminded her that her wild Wednesday had been a long swoosh, not a quick dip). Her partner shifted work times and her mum came over twice a week. A team effort indeed.

As she was recovering, Alice started to feel strong enough to dive into leadership again. Now an interim CEO in a local youth project covering maternity leave, she was still eager to learn and had signed up for a regional meeting with other civil society leaders. It felt good to be part of that community of aspiring good leaders.

The cloud spotter may see a silver lining around a cloud. Those with a spiritual perspective may say, 'Smile at your difficulties,' or 'Embrace your suffering.' The activist may say, 'Let rage be your fuel.' Those with a more practical inclination may just say, 'Make the best of a bad job.' However you say it, it adds up to much the same: reframe. Take this not as a cheesy aspiration, but as practising a positive mindset to carry you through rainy days.

Alice was always on the lookout for silver linings and she had found one in the form of Grace. With mentor training and rich life experience, Grace had offered to be an online mentor for a first-time CEO and had been paired with Alice, whom she had first met just before she was unceremoniously sacked. Then Grace continued to support her to recover and get moving again. After six months they had wrapped up their mentoring relationship with a warm virtual hug and with all best wishes for whatever lay ahead.

For on-it Alice, things had moved quickly, but Grace, who had maintained a professional boundary in their relationship, not sharing her own dramas, still had more swampland ahead. Wading through her own mud, Grace had nevertheless found that giving had been twice blessed ('Shakespeare says it best,' she said) and that she was richly rewarded by the experience of offering a hand into raging wild waters to help a civil society colleague.

Then came a day, more or less half a year after she and Grace had ended their mentoring relationship, when Alice was on her way to meet a local funder, that a breeze blew. It was an actual breeze that moved the trees and was also the kind that was a quiet voice in her head. That breeze voice told her to turn the steering wheel left, not right, so she did. She had time to spare, no problem. The little voice told her to park her car and take a walk through the park. So she did.

And so it was that her breeze inside blew her into the queue in a park café with a warm not-far-from-the-end-of-the-week kind of buzz in the air. All sorts of tasty drinks were vying for her attention.

'Anything with your latte?' tempted the polite barista. Eyeing the pastries from her vantage point now at the head of the queue, Alice reckoned she deserved a Thursday treat. Why not? Mystified by the turn of events but surprisingly untroubled, she smiled at her good fortune as a message told her, with fulsome apologies for very short notice, that regrettably the meeting to which she had been heading, had, due to unforeseen circumstances, been cancelled. *Too bad*, she thought, and with a broadening smile, *that's alright then, isn't it.*

Alice and Grace (share a container)

The barista popped a sweet rocky road chocolate brownie on a plate. *A rocky road indeed*, thought Alice. Hers had been. As a Thursday treat the café added coloured smarties all over their homemade brownies. *My rocky road has a silver lining today*, thought Alice, mixing her metaphors as she often did.

Surprised, but (knowing this was a day of happy chances) content to accept whatever came her way, Alice spotted a familiar face relaxing in the comfy chair by the window. Sitting there all calm and collected was Grace, her mentor. Alice smiled and sent up a thank you. Her lucky angel was indeed with her today.

And so it was, in a buzzy café on a Thursday morning, that Grace and Alice found themselves physically face to face for the first time. In three dimensions Alice was taller than Grace had seen her on screen, and three-dimensional Grace was shorter in person than Alice had imagined.

Comfy chairs, camomile, coffee and rocky roads to share, they relished the moment.

Only loosely held by the boundaries of their now-ended mentoring relationship, they each spoke about what had come to pass when they were in their wild waters times.

When it's over, it's not over. The noise has stopped but the echoes roll on while a new phase starts that's less rocky but still perilous. A year after our wild waters time, we are closer to coping but full recovery is a way off.

You know it's not over for you when many months later you overhear a random remark that pokes you in the ribs and pushes you into dark despair. That can happen. You may be in another leadership position when unintegrated trauma resurfaces. The past has power over us because that past lives in us.

Like training for a physical challenge, it's in the rest times that the body gets stronger, not when you are running at full stretch. The recovery phase is an opportunity, if we so choose, to allow ourselves to feel the pain, to grieve. We may embrace it, digest and integrate the experience, and with that we may renew.

Alice shared the distress she had felt before deciding to do what she knew would help her through, like finding a wild swimming community. Her partner, who had meanwhile become so enraged by events that she was edging towards becoming more part of the problem than the solution, robustly had told Alice to take herself in hand.

Grace shared how she had benefitted from volunteering and also how she had felt lost and on her own. She owned up to what she saw as her transgressions and unhelpful habits; facing them, she said, had helped her embrace them and move on.

Taken back to those rocky days after she had become the third of three CEOs to depart, Alice said, 'I just needed someone, something to hold me somehow. It felt like the ground was giving way under my feet. Nothing to hold.' Looking around, Alice saw the floor, the ceiling, the wall and all that they contained, and for a moment imagined everything around her – the walls, the windows, the ceiling, the chairs, everything solid – evaporating like the morning mist, leaving her sitting on a chair suspended in nothingness.

The comfy chair was still holding her, but she imagined everything around her was no longer there. That's how it had felt a year ago. All that had seemed solid had faded away to become anything but. She drifted, surrounded by nothing.

No longer bound by the constraint of their now closed mentoring relationship, Grace felt at liberty to share her own story. Comfortably seated, she and Alice strolled together down their respective rocky roads, each finding a willing listener in the other. They found that recounting these past dramas brought a twist of a smile. They looked back on those blurry days that followed those dark disturbing nights and felt a warm glow that they had both found the resolve to do what needed to be done.

Although different ages, their stories had played out with different characters; they shared a lot. 'We all have much more in common,' they agreed, 'if you open your eyes and care to see it.'

Grace's faith had given her some kind of grounding and had held her. But her faith had been profoundly shaken when all parties had claimed God to be on their side, and she found herself unsure of what she had previously held as incontrovertible truth.

During her time of struggle, she had been blessed by the company of an old college friend who somehow had been able to hold her in her turmoil. She had contained without pushing, challenging or demanding. She was just there, listening, offering a container like the walls, floor and ceiling that held her now.

The old college friend was a wise woman who knew how to be there and listen deeply, not denying her own struggles, but also being able to rise beyond and see through them, to be fully with another, to be present. She had herself been through desperate times, had come out the other end and her pain had become her resource.

'LEADS' is an easy thing to remember for leaders:

Listen deeply (with no interruption)

Embrace (take in) what we hear

Articulate (meaning) to ourselves, and then

Decide if this is a good moment to

Share (with the person you are listening to)

When we are present, we feel what's happening in us at the same time as we feel what's happening in the other. Our presence is a gift to the other and for ourselves.

Listening to the birds, taking the neighbour's dog for a spin round the block, feeding the ducks, breathing the damp fresh air of the evening woods, had put Grace's struggles into perspective and made them easier to live with. She had found her solid ground within.

When life serves up woe, makes sure you get lots of WOE: drink enough Water, get Outside to breathe fresh air, and Exercise. Try scribbling a daily WOE note so you can follow your progress.

While your physical body is benefitting from the water you are drinking, you may like to spare a moment's thought for the symbolism of water – it connects all people, everywhere on Earth, sustaining life since the beginning of time.

As she heard about how Grace had been supported by her wise woman friend and by nature through the drama of the new Chair, Alice started to become philosophical, poetic even, about life's challenges. A broken heart opens the way to love again… the rainy day brings fresh green grass… every tense exchange opens the way for forgiveness and understanding… the more nourishing the ground and the stronger the roots, the stronger the tree trunk will be and with that come stronger branches and more fruit… She could have continued, there was more.

Through moistening eyes and with a shaky voice, Grace smiled and said, 'What on earth did they put in that rocky road?'

Noticing Grace's emotional display, a new arrival grabbing a moment out of the office threw a glance in her direction and told the barista, 'I'll have what she's having,' unaware of the full price Grace had paid over the past year.

With a triple-shot macchiato, the power-dressed woman rushed back to her office to carry on her crazy day, picking up a ready meal on the way. This flying visitor, who was permanently racing between meetings and domestic duties, longed for respite and had yet to learn the skill of creating space to breathe.

Bob and Daniel (are on screen)

'Look at the time!' The morning calm was shifting into a lunchtime throng with its lengthening queue of tense expressions. 'A funny thing, time,' said Alice. 'We've been back over a whole year in just a couple of hours. Time flies when you're having fun.'

Grace smiled. 'And it drags when you're not. When I was in my wild waters time, I thought it would never end. Everything seemed impossible. It was hard to get to the end of the day. Every small thing I had to do felt like climbing a mountain, even silly little things like doing the washing up or fixing a time for a meeting. But now I'm looking back on it, it all looks different, like a nightmare in a bubble that's slowly fading into the past.'

When you are in raging wild water it seems endless. But it *will* end, sooner or later and, in the grand scheme of things, probably sooner. But it doesn't seem that way when you are up to your neck in it. But when you look back you will see it as a time of your life that came, raged and went.

As they began to gather their things to leave, they were eyed eagerly by those who would gladly rest themselves in those comfy chairs by the window, innocent of the dramatic stories the chairs had been containing for the best part of the morning. The comfy chairs were ready and waiting to bear the burden of the next round of human dramas.

Alice and Grace said their fond farewells and Grace set off back towards the park and home. She carried with her the spirit of Saint B and she sensed that all would be well when she was back at work the following week. Their rocky road exchanges had rekindled in her the belief in the spirit of all that's good in the not-for-profit sector and those many who work in and live for a decent and civil society.

Enriched by their conversations, Alice manoeuvred her way through the loud lunchtime chatter to the back of the café for a quick pitstop on the way to her car. She mused upon how much of a gift a cancelled meeting can turn out to be.

A sudden crash smash of crockery was followed by a shocked hush in the lunchtime throng, and all eyes turned towards the reddening barista with a 'Trainee' badge. Oh dear.

In that momentary hush, Alice felt an impulse to stop. So she did. Then a quiet voice said, 'Look up,' so she did.

Maybe you hear a whisper, like a little bird twittering in your ear, or a gentle nudge in the ribs. Stop. The signal is tiny, but the message could be massive. Perhaps you overhear something, maybe a conversation on the bus, in the street or on television. It touches you and you hear echoes throughout the day. As quiet as it is, this weak signal, this inkling of an idea, could be sending an important message to you. Notice it.

This is a true 'whisper' story. One day in 1980 as I was riding to work, a quiet yet persistent voice told me to stop my motorbike and knock on the door of a big house in west London and ask if I could live there. It was a fine building, next to a park. The voice made no sense, but I couldn't ignore it. I stopped, walked over to the house and knocked on the door. It was the Centre for Biodynamic Therapy.

Following the weak signal that day opened many doors for me that led me to years of psychotherapy training, lifelong friendships, to meeting my wife, having kids and... well, that's another story...

Alice blinked. How many happy chances can one person have in one day? She couldn't believe her eyes. There above her was a television, no sound, but with flashing subtitles: '... knife crime... gangs...

estates…' Then on the TV appeared a calm, composed and self-assured Bob. Yes, the Bob she knew. Stopped short, Alice turned to an innocent bystander and heard herself say, 'I know him, he's the bloke who ran a course I was on.' Innocent bystander smiled faintly. 'Oh really? That's nice.'

Indeed it was, for Alice. Nice, very nice. As she was studying the subtitles, another character appeared on screen: 'Daniel Jones, Chair.'

Alice remembered the course when trainer Bob had said how having a solid relationship with your board is as important as breathing and other life-sustaining pastimes. Always to the point, he had said, 'Mess that up and you're screwed.' The TV subtitles read: 'Mess that up and you're scarred.' *Yes, and yes*, thought Alice.

'Good board relationships, especially with your CEO call for intention, attention and daily hard work,' said Daniel wisely. 'That's it, just do it, no messing,' said Bob. 'We wanted to create an atmosphere not of division but of inspiration,' they both said.

Like any relationship in which the parties have taken a commitment, the Chair/CEO relationship must be cultivated with intention and constant attention. The intention is to do all that can be done to advance the common ambition to deliver the organization's mission, based on shared values. It also means bringing the attention, with the goodwill, time and energy that will enrich it. Add patience, courage and forgiveness into the mix, and a Chair and a CEO will indeed be a dynamic and powerful force for positive change.

Now there they were, side by side on lunchtime TV being interviewed. A dynamic duo indeed. Alice, with the café clatter rising again, having recovered from the crockery crash, noticed their confident demeanours and was transfixed by the rolling subtitles. This was an example to follow; she knew she could believe in better.

She was amazed to read their story of how they had pulled themselves back from the 'edge of the cliff' as Daniel put it, below which, they both said, were raging wild waters. Each in their own ways had been sorely troubled by it all. They both saw the very present danger of splitting and had decided to focus on what they had in common, not on their differences. Each said the other had made the first move to start the difficult conversation and rebuild trust; both agreed it didn't really matter who had taken the initiative.

Bob, CEO, and Daniel, Chair, had agreed to meet for a coffee, in person, no matter where, just as long as they could meet face to face, eye to eye. That first conversation was hard for both of them, calling for all the courage they could muster and, they both said, a lot of listening, understanding and some forgiveness. They each had their own bit of the truth and the whole truth lay between them.

The hardest part of any difficult conversation is to start. Caught by your own turmoil you go over and over what might happen. What will they say... I don't have time today... what will come next? Be courageous. Pick up the phone, write that email.

We can learn from great leaders, although their struggle was on a different scale to ours. Carrying the burden of decades of racial injustice, Nelson Mandela and F.W. de Klerk met for the first time. With the great weight of history on their shoulders, they met, according to Mandela's account, 'just as two men'. Finding the courage to take the first step opened the way to resolving entrenched conflict.[16]

As the months passed and they hauled themselves back from the cliff edge, Bob and Daniel came up with a cunning plan about how they would handle media, this being the most critical flashpoint between them. They both liked being in front of the camera and the mic and were equally good at it.

There it was on the subtitles: 'Well,' said Daniel, 'we agreed I'd take the lead on the bad-news stories and Bob would take the lead on the good-news stories. If it was going to be controversial or difficult, I should be fronting it as Chair.' 'That works for me,' said Bob with a grin.

---

[16] Nelson Mandela *The Long Walk to Freedom* (1994).

With skill and the good of the organization close at heart, they had managed to create a friendly professional relationship that was visible to all. Time passed, two trustees resigned citing personal matters, but actually meaning they still couldn't get behind Bob, and slowly the dangerous icy split on the board started melting. Moving back from the brink called for all the compassion, courage and wisdom that Daniel and Bob could muster.

Staff had started noticing what was happening and, like a ripple passing across water from a thrown pebble, it soon reached their daily interactions. It started to show up in little ways. Someone brought a cake for a birthday and others did the same, they started showing some interest in colleagues' holiday plans and helping those who had personal struggles, not least by offering a listening ear. They were not becoming close friends, but as colleagues they were finding ways to be kind and friendly.

Followers who believe in better and choose good leaders to lead them will inevitably be disappointed – because good leaders do their best, which is rarely perfect. And followers will see good leaders work to put things right when things fall apart.

Alice (is believing in better)

In awe, Alice gazed open-mouthed at this Chair and CEO whom she knew had once been in deep trouble. After a brief honeymoon, they hadn't hit it off at all and were not far from hitting each other with passive aggressive blows to the ego.

But somehow Alice saw that, despite the distance between them, and most courageously, they had pulled themselves back from the brink and got themselves together. She marvelled at the change, actually a transformation, and wanted to know what had happened.

Some months later she would discover that Daniel, in the moment of his greatest desperation about the situation, had met with his older brother who had offered sound advice. Actually, it wasn't him but their mother, who, although long gone, was still present for them both and whose voice Daniel heard so clearly that he felt her presence right behind him, quiet words in his ear. These were words he had been carrying with him all his life.

His mother's voice was as alive as ever to him: 'It's your job to steady the ship, keep things on an even keel. You live up to your name, my Daniel, God will be your judge.'

Daniel and his brother had smiled at their mother's memory, recalling how many of her wise words related back to the momentous time in her life so many decades ago when she had sailed to England to start a new life, since when the family had been awash with sea-going metaphors, some sage, some silly, all memorable.

From that moment with his brother, Daniel had resolved to do better, to think and act differently, to do all he could to pour oil on troubled waters, to steady the ship. He knew he couldn't sidestep things anymore but had to face up to facts, starting with a talk with Bob, straight and simple.

The harsh truth of Alice's own failed CEO/Chair relationship was still casting a long shadow over the hopeful story on screen played out in rolling subtitles. What a contrast. She still bore the scars of her dismissal after the long and turbulent year since the fateful interview when she hadn't looked before she leapt.

She had heard through the grapevine that 'her' Chair, Sarah, had hung on, repeatedly saying she would stand down when the time was right. But the time, apparently, was never right. Quite.

Alice found she had an unhealthy interest in what had happened after she left and was disturbed to discover that she was not entirely unhappy when she heard that things hadn't been going well – she didn't like that side of herself.

Some of us, sometimes, find an unwanted sense of pleasure in the misfortune of others. English has imported the German word 'Schadenfreude'.

Happily, there's a way of responding – a life's work. Along with love, compassion and equanimity, we may try practising 'sympathetic joy' when we notice we are falling into envy and resentment on noticing the good fortune of others. Along with embracing our own suffering when it comes along, we may practise seeing Schadenfreude not as a distasteful obstacle in us, but rather accepting it, standing back, looking into it and seeking to understand its origins within us. *Endnote²¹*

Early in her relationship with her Chair, Alice had thought it was going so well. Until the day she dug into the accounts, and it dawned on her that there wasn't enough money to pay for her salary. It was a bit of a shock to say the least, actually pretty devastating. She still bitterly regretted that she hadn't asked questions at the interview and since then had been living by the look-before-you-leap mantra that she had first heard a couple of years before.

With furrowed brow, Alice remembered Sarah's sudden interest in recycled bags and pens emblazoned with the charity's logo and 'Believe in Better' all over them, and how she had dashed off with barely a word with Alice or anyone, and had got them designed and produced with no thought for what they would be used for. This was to be a bitter lesson about the blurring of the boundary between governance and operations that was to serve Alice well in her career for years to come.

She remembered her uneasy feeling when she discovered that one member of her team was the daughter of one of Sarah's best friends with whom she met every month for tea and chat. She discovered that neither the team colleague, nor her mother, nor Sarah had maintained any kind of firewall, so Alice too often found that information that should have been contained between CEO and Chair or CEO and team was flying all around the houses, almost literally.

Troubled though she was, Alice was so inspired by Daniel and Bob that she was encouraged to do better in her next job, starting with believing in better right away. (Whoever had come up with the wording on the conference bag two years before would never know the good things that flowed from their efforts.)

Know that your every word and act will show up someday, somewhere. Know that you can't escape the consequences of your actions and also that you will never know the full impact they will have, for good or ill.

So Alice resolved to get out there and live life to the full with courage and determination, and to exercise due diligence in so doing. *What would AI say?* she wondered. 'Tell me the ten most important things to do to build a good relationship between CEO and Chair of a charity,' she dictated into her phone and waited a few moments for AI's response. Alice was on-it and was busily ripening as a good leader.

No point falling off a cliff into wild waters, she reasoned. Look before you leap. Yes indeed.

Board members, Chair, CEOs, senior team – do your due diligence, meaning that you have enough information about what you might be getting into. Look at the money, the quality of governance process and the people who you would be working with, especially the key players. Be diligent or (probably) be sorry. *Endnote*[22]

Bob (feeling the fear and doing it anyway)

Dazzled and inspired by what she had seen played out on the screen, Alice took her leave of the café to drive back to the office. Just as she was wondering whether this might turn out to be a day of happy chances, she felt an urge to 'Call Bob'. They had exchanged phone numbers on the course a couple of years ago.

Voices inside her said, *I can't do that... yes you can... he won't remember me... what am I going to say... maybe he's changed his number...* The loudest voice said, *Oh shut up Alice, just do it.*

She pulled over and, with phone in one hand and courage in both, she dialled his number. To her amazement Bob answered. Only two rings and she heard his voice.

'Hello Al, how you doin'?' Knowing that no one could get him back, Bob had developed a habit of abbreviating names with more than one syllable. And he had just left the TV studio and was full of it. 'Yes,' he said, 'you're calling at a good time, and yes, I'd love to chat.'

A happy chance, Alice's third today.

Bob's side of the story tumbled out. He said he had come a long way in two long years from those early days when he jumped in with his big boots and started grabbing all those juicy media opportunities.

'All good to start with, then things went weird, off the rails. Team was with me, mainly, but some playing silly buggers, board all over the place. It was all getting pretty heavy. I was about to chuck it. I'd had enough of all that rollocks,' he confessed.

'Just when I was about to pack it in, I got a call from Daniel.' (Bob resisted the temptation to call him Dan out of respect.) 'He said, "We need to talk," straight and simple. I was guessing this was going to be a "the board has lost confidence in you, goodbye" kind of conversation. But it wasn't. He wanted to meet. I put on my big boy's pants and turned up at the meeting. Feel the fear and do it anyway.' Bob laughed, not knowing quite where the phrase came from.

'"Go on Bob," I said to myself, "You're a big boy now, be as big as you are." Just Daniel and me it was.'

There's no time like the present to face up to the irritations that may arise between you and colleagues. It may be to do with who is leading what or about when and how it's acceptable to contact each other. Own up to those tiny-but-can-easily-get-big irritations like agreeing how good news and bad news will be handled. Agree what will happen when things go wrong and under what circumstances you can be contacted for 'urgent matters' out of 'normal working hours'.

It was a bumpy start but finding his fears to be unfounded, Bob had levelled with his Chair, confessed his enthusiasm for being in the limelight and managed to find the generosity in himself to apologize for overdoing it. He had said he wanted them to work out a way to do this together. And that's exactly what they did, while the rumbles from those who hadn't supported his appointment in the first place grumbled on.

They learned to admit the strength of their own egos and say what had been just too hard to say to each other previously. Not only that, but Daniel let the whole board in on their discussions. Everything was put on the table. No hiding.

Being of one mind that failure wasn't an option, and that rocky board and staff dynamics were too hot to handle on their own, they decided to get help. They hired a qualified facilitator who earned their trust at their very first meeting, listening patiently to their stories. He was open, authentic, curious, asked incisive questions and dared to speak the truth, calmly, fully and as needed. They both especially liked that he was genuinely engaged, didn't hide behind management blah-di-blah and said he would create a process that was not some ill-fitting off-the-shelf standard method but one that would 'fit like a glove'.

A turbulent and stuck group dynamic is one of many good reasons to engage a group process facilitator. Maybe there's a muddle in which things don't make sense, or you notice you get easily provoked by otherwise insignificant comments. Maybe people are taking sides on the board and chatter in cliques. These are symptoms of unspoken conversations that arise from a hidden group dynamic.

A facilitator will listen, understand and safely 'hold the space' for that deeper turbulence to safely come up for air and to find resolution.

The facilitator proposed three meetings over a few weeks and suggested a process for each meeting, all the time adapting and shifting according to the dynamic as it unfolded. The change of place and the change of pace, he had suggested, would be a powerful combination.

With their resolve to see the bigger picture and to work for the best, together with the skills and insight of an independent third person, they got through it, difficult moments and all. They found that snuggled within the plain truth that the board leads on longer-term strategy and the CEO leads operations, is tricky dark matter.

Those in-between things that could equally well be for the board or for the CEO is tricky dark matter that can drag you down into an abyss of irritation. They are those areas of activity that could just as well be seen as strategy or operations, so look at them together and decide on which side of the line they fall. Such things will then be rendered neither tricky nor dark.

There were some heated and many memorable healing moments in those sessions, which culminated with them agreeing a 'scheme of delegation' to include who of the Chair, trustees and CEO would lead on what. They not only agreed the 'what' but also 'how' they would work together (like Bob knowing that Daniel was a stickler for proper punctuation and Daniel knowing not to contact Bob on a Saturday, which was his football and mates day).

Like a hawk (or indeed an African fish eagle hovering high above the Usutu river), a Chair hovers so high up that everyday operations are not visible. When necessary, and alongside the CEO, the Chair may zoom in to take a look at what's going on at ground level. But most of the time the hawk is to be found floating gracefully with full attention, far above it all with eyes to the far horizon.

When Daniel and Bob brought the scheme of delegation to the board for formal approval, their fellow trustees put their cynicism aside, saw the change and soon started referring to them as the 'dynamic duo'. They had found a way of playing to their strengths – one bringing a broad perspective, including his memory of the stories he had heard from his mum about their struggles when they arrived in the UK in the 1950s, the other first-hand knowledge of the multicultural cut and thrust of life on rough estates.

Rose (shouts her colourful expletives at a mountain)

That same Thursday, indeed at that same moment, they were shouting out their anger at the silent slopes and laughed as colourful expletives echoed through the majesty of the mountains. Stamping their feet, they raged gleefully and the age-old rock took their pain. They sang 'Blackbird' and shouted even louder when they got to '… take these broken wings and learn to fly…' Endnote[23]

By happy chance, Rose's lifelong friend – who had been overwhelmed for too many years and had also just resigned her job as headteacher – had managed to persuade her to head for the hills. Not just any old hills down the road but faraway mountains in America.

'A good dose of faraway fresh air, that's what we need. Let's go.'

When the time comes to leave a job, draw a bold firm line. Whether it's 24 years, 24 months or weeks, happily or unhappily, sooner or later you will get to the point when it's time to go. When that ending comes, whatever the circumstances, let go... and go. This opens the way for 'letting come'. Whether you are a Chair, board member, CEO, founder, senior team member, draw a line and boldly embark on the new. Do it absolutely.

They knew in their bones that being physically distant from the challenging experience was going to help their healing. It was a necessary adventure to boldly go where they hadn't gone before, far away, and to blast out their troubles.

Remembering the therapy groups of their younger years, they knew the relief of catharsis. Rose had been helped by a coach whom she had first spoken with during those difficult crisis days a year ago. Her coach had been there when needed, not at fixed times, and Rose carried the thought of their sessions up the mountains (easily carried, unlike the backpack). To start with, sessions had been frequent, then fewer, then every month or two. But Rose knew he would be there until they agreed that they had arrived at 'the end of the chapter'.

Our crises, unlike African rivers, are not of known length but may flow for a couple of months, maybe a year or more. But, like every river, they will surely come to an end.

Although I can make guesses about what will unfold, there will be unexpected twists and turns on the way. I follow the unfolding process.

Gazing over the spectacular valley, Rose remembered the painful struggle both within herself and with her board. After dozens, actually hundreds, of emails, lawyers' letters and broken nights, Rose had left with a settlement: cash in the bank, an adequate reference and an agreed statement for internal and external consumption. She had been uncomfortable about taking the charity's reserves, which she and her team had worked so hard to build up.

A settlement agreement is a complex and important document. If there's anything you don't understand, ask your lawyer. Do not sign with eyes closed and fingers crossed.

Rose was pragmatic and knew that it would take her some time to recover from the emotional tumble dryer she had been through, but up on that mountain top she was buoyed by a sense that the best was yet to come.

A SUMMIT

Rose had managed to settle with her conscience and then with her board. She needed a financial buffer to carry her to the point where she could get back on track. As the settlement was tax free and as she was always careful with her money, she reckoned she would have funds to sustain her for a while.

On her way to the mountains, she realized that letting go of the painful memories of the settlement had been much harder than handing back her laptop and other bits of accumulated kit to which she knew she had become over-attached. Her lingering memories had a nasty habit of poking her in the ribs: words overheard in a bus queue, something in the news, an arty poster in the street were all mini-triggers that could upset her day.

But with her good friend, who had her own story to tell, she had marched herself up the mountain and then marched herself down again, and after all their shouting, stamping and raging over the unyielding rock, her memories were gradually robbed of their sting. 'Better out than in,' they screamed. They had taken themselves in hand and were healing.

Given time and attention, most individual and collective trauma will fade, at least disappearing from view. If you take care of your wounds as you would a cut on your finger, they will heal more quickly and more deeply. Notice, accept, embrace, understand, be free. Be a committed agent in your own recovery and discovery. Take care of yourself by sniffing out what nourishes your body, heart and soul while you seek to understand – a walk in the park, a quiet coffee with a friend, maybe the view from the top of a faraway hill.[17]

---

[17] Thomas Hübl *Healing Collective Trauma: A Process for Integrating Our Intergenerational and Cultural Wounds* (2020).

On the way through your recovery you may find that you have an unconscious driver that's constantly, well, driving you. Some can be helpful, sometimes. But some are unhelpful, so notice them and, if they are no longer serving you, do not feed them.

As the two robust, late-middle-aged women slushed through a mountain bog one day, Rose gave her 'Be Perfect' driver a thorough talking to – she had always struggled with her perfectionist tendencies. She decided to shift to a 'Be Pragmatic' habit. As they quickened their pace, they laughed at how bedraggled they looked on the outside and rejoiced at their inner resolve to turn over a new leaf.

For Rose the end of one life chapter had arrived and a new chapter was about to begin.

Sarah (is holding on too long)

To start with, things had gone well between Sarah and Alice's replacement (who was the fourth CEO, Alice having been the third).

'A terribly charming young man,' she had declared to her friends. 'I think we'll get on very well. He gets on with our little team and has already met with all the other board members. He thinks we should bring in some new people.'

But that was then and this is now. To start with she had thought Alice's replacement was just what the doctor ordered, but after a few months she noticed that things were changing.

'It wasn't easy, you know. He said we needed a Vice-Chair to stand in for me if I couldn't be there. We all thought it seemed fair enough. Then the next thing I knew was that one of the new board members had been appointed as Vice-Chair at a meeting I couldn't get to because the barn was flooded. Most distressing.'

That had been a few months previously. It had all become rather unpleasant, with secret emails and texts, and conversations in corners. Alice's replacement and the new Vice-Chair had been getting on very well.

The Vice-Chair had suggested they meet to 'talk about a few things'. It was to be later that very afternoon and Sarah wasn't looking forward to the conversation one little bit.

Meanwhile, the team knew something was up and asked themselves, *What about me?* which is the question asked by most of us in turbulent times.

Over breakfast, her perceptive husband could see which way things were going. 'Give me a call after the meeting will you darling?' He knew what was coming.

Tara and Imran (invite truth and trust at a board meeting)

Imran's first foray into the nonprofit world hadn't started well. For the best part of the last year he had been tossed about in the wild waters of poor governance. This wasn't what he had imagined a couple of years earlier when he had stumbled across a *Big Issue* seller after a business lunch on his way back to his corporate office.

Brought up to be self-sufficient, hardworking and ambitious, qualities that his parents had brought with them from Mumbai to Manchester, he had always imagined that charities were run by some other breed of person, not plagued by those human frailties that he saw every day in his world of investment banking. Surely charity people had 'decency' written all through them like a stick of Brighton rock?

And here was Imran the morning before chairing his first board meeting as Acting Chair, readying himself to walk through the agenda with Tara the CEO. He had been knocked about by his experiences and knew Tara, who was due any minute, had taken a battering too.

Imran recalled how he had been engaged soon after the new Chair had been recruited following an external process. The new Chair had been impressed by Imran when he saw him speak at an investor event and found himself surprised that such a young man could shine.

Momentarily putting to one side his prejudice of which he was barely and rarely aware, the new Chair had called him one sunny morning and invited him to join the board of his heritage charity. Other trustees knew this wasn't the right way of recruiting but said nothing. 'Smart young guy, good with money, seems like a good fit, will add a bit of colour to proceedings,' he said to a couple of other board members, and to Imran he said, 'My dear old grandfather set up that charity, you know. He was a local businessman. Some liked him, some didn't. Anyway, a good chap. You're just what we need. Are you in?'

His question had a sharp twist to it. 'No is not the required answer,' he had quipped while Imran was reflecting on how to respond.

Once upon a time, an informal 'tap on the shoulder' recruitment was commonplace. No longer; it's poor practice.

From that moment it had been a bumpy ride for Imran. Had he tempered his enthusiasm to step up and do something charitable and had done his due diligence, as was his regular practice in business, he might not have succumbed so readily to this new Chair's robust charms.

Imran's journey into the world of civil society had started a couple of years before when he had been inspired by the animated chatter of a crowd spilling onto the street at a charity conference. That momentary spark had reminded him of his parents, who told him to live the five pillars, especially alms-giving. After a brief spell of volunteering with a homeless charity he had decided it was time to do more.

'Oh well, that was then and now is now. No good going over old ground,' he said. 'That new Chair is now a departed Chair and it's time for a fresh start.' That's exactly what was needed, starting with today's board meeting. Shaking on the inside, Imran successfully conveyed an air of calm confidence on the outside.

Tara arrived with apologies for being a few minutes late.

'No problem,' said Imran. 'Look, before we get to the board meeting, I think we need to go over everything that's been happening. It's not been easy, has it?'

Tara readily agreed.

So there they were, both diving back into the wild waters they had been through. Imran knew that it hadn't been so bad for him, but for Tara this had been an existential crisis that had put her job at risk and hadn't done anything for her health either. He knew they needed to clear the air.

They acknowledged that things had been building up for a while. From day one the previous Chair had been a divisive influence. His modus operandi was to control by pushing himself forward, openly criticizing Tara and sending long emails about operational details, demanding immediate replies. Divide and rule had worked well for him so far, why not now?

An elephant in the room suffocates. A shark or crocodile will bite your legs off. Look out for all such uninvited guests in the meeting room.

A handful of the board members had succumbed to the now-departed Chair's ego, indeed were submerged by it, and allowed themselves to be drawn into cabals of intrigue while he discouraged CEO Tara from having any contact with new trustees ('I'll speak to them, don't worry').

Meanwhile, the other trustees had looked the other way, sat on their hands and had either not responded to Tara's increasingly exasperated messages or were vaguely supportive in a non-committal kind of way. The Treasurer simply disappeared from view.

There's trouble brewing and we hope it will just go away. Well it probably won't. Tactical waiting might be best, but it's more likely to be simple avoidance.

One thing you can do is not gossip within your own little echo chamber but find the courage to say what you know needs to be said and to the right people, who might not be the easiest people to deal with.

One board member had invited Tara for coffee and spilled out her own concerns about the Chair's behaviour, while another sent dark late-night emails about bullying. Another met the Chair for lunch and tried, with little success, to talk with him.

Imran, a perceptive character, could see what was happening and had done his best to steer a middle course through the divide; quiet diplomacy was his way. Such behaviour was not the kind that Imran expected at a board table. Although very much the junior, he plucked up the courage to talk to the Chair, but he too didn't get far.

Over Sunday breakfast the previous Chair told his wife, 'They've been going for a hundred years and need solid investment knowhow on the board. Most of the board have been there too long and like to swan about chatting to volunteers in the gardens. I need to build up reserves.'

'Yes dear, how interesting,' offered his wife.

Anyway, it had all came to a head on one not very fine day. A storm in a teacup was provoked by the way the founding of the charity was described on the newly designed website. Tara had been speaking with the much appreciated former Chair, a decent man with integrity and local standing, who had stepped down because of his health. But he was well enough to invite his successor for lunch.

No one knows quite what was said, but the Chair abruptly resigned the next day with little explanation other than something about being a round peg. Maybe he was strong, but he was definitely wrong. Having thrown his hat in the ring a year earlier, he now threw in the towel. Three other board members left soon thereafter, citing business and family pressures.

The board had taken its eye off the ball and had allowed the Vice-Chair position to remain vacant for much too long. The Chair had said he would sort it out, everyone around the table acquiesced and nothing happened. A few mumbled to each other about it but most had got on with the rest of their lives. Mistake! Now it was too late and a gap had suddenly opened up, they realized their error of omission.

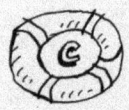

Royalty finds it wise, so it's said, to have an 'heir and a spare'. What's good for royalty is also good for boards. Anything can happen to a Chair that may cause them to be temporarily or permanently absent, so make sure there's a backup. Make sure your board is future-proofed by having a Vice-Chair or perhaps two, each leading on agreed areas of activity and both ready to step up when the need arises.

Having sought the views of all trustees, Tara had asked Imran, to his great surprise, if he would kindly step into the breach and chair this meeting. She could see he was a rising star and valued his integrity and young wisdom.

Despite the disarray of recent months, Tara had made the time to take care of the little things. She had read somewhere that there was a positive correlation between the quality of biscuits on offer at a meeting and participants' level of satisfaction. 'Chocolate biscuits power good meetings' read the pop psychology headline.

Look after the board members' personal needs. At an in-person event, take care of the small things, such as tea, decent coffee and refreshments, or making sure there's mint tea for the person who prefers it. Take care of the person who has a back problem and who needs a more comfortable chair and space to stretch. Whether in person or online, find genuine interest in individual needs and interests (grandchildren, pets, hobbies and the like). Remember birthdays.

The conversation of the few trustees who had already arrived was restrained, as if the whole room was collectively holding its breath. A few were seated and tried to make themselves invisible by gazing intently at their board papers. Although they had all been on the receiving end of the over-directive way that the now-departed Chair had conducted meetings, none of them had said anything. As Imran walked into the room they were nervous, while allowing themselves to be just a little bit hopeful.

I am therefore I meet

I meet therefore I am

Imran was determined to do it differently by talking less and listening more. With determination and trepidation in equal measure on the inside, he conveyed a warm confidence with just a twist of vulnerability on the outside. He had once learned about the power of body language from a senior colleague and knew it wasn't about pretending but about calling on those true inner bits of himself that would meet the moment.

Trust had taken a knocking and he knew he had to rebuild it, not by talking about it but by living it, carefully telling the truth as he knew it and by acting in a way that gradually earned the trust of those around him.

Each time you speak the truth as you know it, you create one more link in the bond of trust between you and those around you. Truth and trust nourish each other.

Robin, Tara and Imran (greet each other with knowing glances)

Tara and Robin had found themselves at the same conference a couple of years previously, when they had sat together and shared their troubles. By a stroke of good fortune they had bumped into each other again a year later when they were in the wildest depths of their wild Wednesday experiences. They recalled their tense conversations of the year before when they hadn't yet noticed that something was brewing.

They propped each other up and offered each other a listening ear and wise counsel as they each navigated their respective raging wild waters. It had been hard, but as the year passed their memories of bad days and dreadful nights were fading.

Tara's new start was the new Chair's sudden exit and Imran filling the gap as Interim Chair.

Robin's new start was accepting he wasn't going to be able to change things and, while stressing about taking charity funds as a settlement, he had eventually signed an agreement and left. He had hung on long enough, actually too long. Time to move on.

Part of the new start he was giving himself was applying for a role as trustee in the heritage charity of which Tara was CEO, and now he was arriving at his first board meeting. Inspired by his nature coaching walk that morning, he was ready for a fresh start and knew he had to resist the temptation of taking the easy way out by rushing into a new job.

There may be a tendency to jump to the next position as a maladaptive way of avoiding the hurt and bolstering a bruised ego. But if you do, you might compound your hurt by repeating and repeating the injustices you feel you have suffered.

You tell yourself how bad it all was, how very bad they were, how silly you were to have done this or that. Full of 'if onlys', you tell your partner, your friends and yourself about how it could have been, if only...

As individuals, as a board or as an organization we are not the first to have ever compulsively repeated our mistakes and pains. Freud named this unconscious tendency 'repetition compulsion', in which we might find ourselves inexplicably re-enacting the event, albeit with different actors, or putting ourselves in situations where the painful event occurs again.

Looking back, Robin realized he should have resigned sooner. As CEO he knew his job was to overcome obstacles, but he had tried once, twice, three and yet more times to fix things and had exhausted himself in the process. He had allowed himself to fall victim to his own driven fantasy that he could fix the unfixable. He had discovered that the hard way and now he had the Serenity Prayer poem hanging on his wall and was learning to 'know the difference'.

As a leader it's essential to develop an understanding of what can be fixed and what can't, and to develop the wisdom of knowing the difference. *Endnote²⁴*

As he arrived in the room, Robin was politely greeted by Imran and he and Tara greeted each other with knowing glances. They both still heard the fading rumble of passing storms and knew that the clean-up should include a proper recruitment process for a new Chair. They had been through tough times and were now stronger from their experiences. This was to be a new beginning for both of them.

Nelson Mandela said, 'Judge me not by my successes but by the number of times I have fallen and picked myself up again.'

Storms pass, headaches pass, crises pass. This moment too has passed; pick yourself up and a new day will surely dawn.

Endings matter. As the crisis passes, the pace and nature of my contact with a coaching client will shift as support is needed less urgently and frequently during recovery. I remain available to meet online or in person, texts, or emails until we agree it is 'the end of the chapter'.

I remain alongside, still open and available but at a distance until closure. At first I was unsure how this arrangement would work out, but in two decades of practice no one has taken advantage.

As things calm, I might make a date to call a while hence or I may be asked to check in after a couple of months. Even if messages go unanswered, nine times out of ten I eventually get a response, with apologies (new phone, been doing this and that, meant to reply but, sorry forgot... etc.).

Until one day we speak and I ask, 'Have we arrived at the end of the chapter?'

Chapter 4
LIFE GOES ON, FIVE YEARS LATER

INTEGRATE, THRIVE

*With courage and determination, all characters
have integrated their traumas and see new horizons...*

UNCHARTED TERRITORIES
(NOT TO SCALE)

Robin

This Friday, in some ways like any other, is special for Robin. Sitting under his favourite oak tree sipping his herbal tea, Robin is in a thoughtful mood.

Over the last five years, he has had a front-row seat to see what 'good' looks like. As a trustee he has seen how CEO Tara and Imran, who was elected as Chair, managed to rebuild trust and professionalism around the table. Robin's eyes have been opened to the possible, and that possible contrasts dramatically with his own board. Under the oak tree he remembers all those years ago when tension went up and his will to live went down.

Looking back, he wonders why he hung on too long. *I've got one life… it's only a job after all.* He has come to realize the obvious truth that he had been ignoring, namely that his time on Earth was short and learning to let go and move on is a key life skill.

He and his worried wife had calculated the settlement money and reckoned that, with care, they could avoid hitting the financial buffers. Now, looking back, it turns out that their sums had been pretty well spot on.

His memory of the nasty illness that struck him down a few months after leaving is fading in the distance. It was horrible. He knows that his body had got its own back for the years of pummelling he had subjected it to. His recovery had hit him hard all over, including, as he told his brother, 'In places I didn't know I had places.' He can laugh at that now.

In the middle of that time, he could do nothing. He had tried to fill out job applications, but every sentence was like climbing a mountain with no oxygen, and the one interview he did get hadn't gone well.

You are not a superhuman. Your body is amazing but not indestructible. You have limits, and crisis helps you find out what they are. When you have been to hell and back it will take some time for your mind and body to rebalance. That job application for a full-time job may have to wait a while, until you have recovered enough. The body, mind and soul overdraft you have accumulated must be repaid.

Robin was simply exhausted. When eventually he realized the obvious, he took himself in hand and set off to walk one of the UK's many long-distance footpaths. Now and again his scratchy exchanges with his board walked with him, as did the wisdoms of his nature coach. The end of all his exploration had indeed been to arrive back at his starting point, sitting under his oak tree as he had done those years before, but now as if for the first time.[18]

Some months later and thankfully well before his settlement monies were spent, he noticed his mojo was gradually returning and some days he felt a renewed flicker of interest in looking for work. He managed a few job applications and, after many rejections ('We had a large number of excellent applications and regret to inform you…') he struck gold.

---

[18] A variation on a theme in T.S. Eliot, 'Little Gidding'.

He upgraded himself from gardening leave to actual gardening. His new job isn't in the hospice movement but in horticulture. Right up his rustic path. This new direction combines his lifelong passion for being out in fresh air with helping people with mental health problems, getting their hands dirty and growing things. It's a small local project, suiting him down to the ground and restoring his depleted energies.

When, 25 years ago, I was in crisis, I felt I was being constantly criticized. Someone said to me, 'Don't put up with being tolerated, work somewhere where you are celebrated.' I made that happen.

It was an easy train ride to one of the regional offices of the heritage charity that Tara had been running when Robin had first met her at that conference, now a full seven years previously. He is now well into his second term on the board and thrilled to have been asked to be the lead for the new horticultural therapy project set up in partnership with a local community group.

If you want to give time as a volunteer think, *What would I love to be asked to do?* I remember being challenged to ask this question when I was a trustee at England's volunteering infrastructure body. It's a powerful question. Let people know, and what you love is more likely to come your way.

But even though the sun is now shining, it had taken some years for Robin's health to recover. His wife had been full of advice about the latest good thing to come along and steered him relentlessly towards various alternative therapies, including acupuncture and attending to his gut microbiome. Although he still heard echoes of the past, the day finally came when he knew he had turned a corner.

He smiles at his rediscovered passion for magic tricks; this weekend he will be the star turn at his neighbour's fireworks party. As he amuses the crowd, pulling rabbits out of hats and such like, he muses on how his story could have taken a different turn if he had employed the same kind of dexterity with his board seven years earlier when trouble had first started brewing.

Tara

Tara ponders the events that brought her to a front room just round the corner from her old office. Her decluttering microbusiness was earning a name for itself. A couple of days a week, she offered a niche service helping anyone in her hometown to get their stuff sorted. Tara knew the impact of physical environment on people's well-being. It fitted in well with her job share as Head of Collections Services at the county museum.

Her former heritage colleagues saw the museum sector as a natural step, but decluttering seemed a bit odd. But for her it felt like a homecoming – her Irish father had always been fascinated by looking through old stuff and putting it in order: 'No clutter outside, no clutter inside,' was one of his many aphorisms.

Sir Winston Churchill said a lot of things; one of them was: 'We shape our buildings; thereafter they shape us.'

Nancy Kline said, 'A thinking environment says back to you "you matter"'[19]

Tara thinks back to the not-at-all brilliant sweep of events of five years ago when the Chair who had wanted to be 'Chair*man*' had just left, with no handover or proper goodbye, and how Imran had stepped up to preside over his first meeting.

You may be left with painful feelings even long after your wild waters time. Writing a letter to the person who has wronged you, even if you never send it, could help you regain perspective. (You will probably need several drafts.)

This had been a turbulent transition in which Tara saw how Imran, with courage, wisdom and charm, had set about rebuilding the board.

Together they had managed to navigate the charity into calmer waters, which was now steered by a strong and competent board. It had been time to move on and now she was loving the variety of her portfolio career.

---

[19] Nancy Kline *Time to Think: Listening to Ignite the Human Mind* (1999).

The spirit of a meeting can be invited to shift from being a 'me-thing' to being a 'we-thing'. Invite the collective.

Her wild waters time and new career direction supercharged her interest in her joint Irish/Asian ancestry. As well as researching her family tree on both sides as far as she could go, she found herself pondering what lives would come to pass seven generations hence – a challenging thought indeed. *Endnote*[25]

Tara had survived the turbulent times quite well, but her partner had been sick with worry about it all and struggled through his chiropractic training, a new career choice.

They were troubled and amused that they had both had versions of the same recurrent nightmare of drowning in rough and rising seas. As the years passed and they were assured of two solid enough incomes, they had made it to calmer waters. Their panicked wakings became fewer and lost their sting, and they were able to laugh when one of them had one of 'those dreams'. She's now proudly satisfied that she hung in there through it all, left when she chose and could look back with a sense of a job well done.

She joined the board of a local charity caring for a stretch of a 300-year-old canal. It's used by dog walkers, runners and wandering souls whose troubles keep them awake at night.

Tara puts her traumatic experience to good use by being the very best trustee she can be; she often smiles at her wild waters time, knowing it has made her stronger and wiser and has led her to find a new form of her life calling.

Worked with and worked through, the suffering that comes our way can become one of our assets, helping us develop wisdom, courage and compassion and then we are more able to be of service to others. 'No Mud, No Lotus'. If there was no messy mud, we would never see the magnificent lotus.

'The way out is in'. Thích Nhất Hạnh suggests that the way to settle the struggles outside us is to explore inside ourselves.

Endnote[26]

Grace

As she presses the red 'End Meeting for All' button, Grace has a sense of calm. Helping other charity leaders to navigate their wild waters is now her way and she knows that this end-of-the-week coaching session has helped the person online. It feels satisfying for her too.

She had always wanted to leave her job at the time of her choosing to draw on what she had learned from her coaching training some years before. Two years after her wild waters time, it was her moment to move on.

A lifelong church member, she had for many years been thinking about training as a Baptist lay minister, but the shine had faded, and the idea didn't inspire her anymore. She wondered about becoming a magistrate but on closer inspection she found little inspiration there either.

Joining an online 'island of sanity' small group where we listen quietly and speak from the heart can warm us and help us to discover our truth.

It had taken six months to clear up the rubble, but the team had pulled together and the job was done thoroughly and well. When Grace was in the middle of her confrontations with her board, it had felt like a world war had broken out, but now she could see it in perspective, as a local skirmish.

Considering her experience and *the* age, with its multiple disruptions of which climate breakdown troubled her the most, she wanted to break the mould, to spread her wings and to put her heart and soul fully into whatever she did. Looking back with a deep sense of gratitude for the joys and suffering she had experienced, Grace knew this was time for a bigger change and to discover peace within.

Practice the '4 Rs' of 'Deep Adaptation': Resilience (keep what we value), Relinquishment (let go), Restoration (what can we bring back to help us), Reconciliation (make peace). *Endnote[27]*

Being cautious, Grace had saved up before giving notice, so she had funds behind her in case it all went wrong. She found that getting her head down and applying to international charities helped focus her attention; they all asked for the same kind of information, so she did lots of cut and paste.

From six applications she got three interviews and one offer – an interim position with a Christian health charity in Africa building infrastructure and capacity, which was looking for maturity and a solid track record. A fresh start indeed. Within one month of her leaving do (at which many fine words were expressed in which only oblique reference was made to the struggles of a few years before) she was on a field trip to East Africa meeting development volunteers.

Her Tanzanian adventure had served her well and she had served the country well for a couple of years until it was time to return home. Although she has no formal coaching qualification she's now much called upon by leaders who know of her experiences and who appreciate her accumulated and hard-won wisdom.

Her wild waters time propelled her into doing 'the work' in weekly psychotherapy sessions, which afforded her the time she needed for reflection, looking inside and gaining insight into the deeper recesses of her unconscious. Having integrated her own traumas, she was able to forgive and has become a remedy for others.[20]

Readying herself for the next coaching call, she now looks back on her time of struggle from which she emerged bruised and full of resolve to do better for herself and the world. As she was in her wild waters time, Grace is still on a mission to stand up for what's right and is determined not to tumble so far down the rabbit hole again.

---

[20] Desmond Tutu *No Future Without Forgiveness* (2000).

Each time you think of something you are grateful for, write it on a slip of paper and put in a jar by the door. Think gratitude every time you brush your teeth.

Sarah

'We'll wait a couple of minutes and then make a start,' says Sarah. A local mover and shaker, and being good at meeting powerful people, she was the obvious choice to chair the group campaigning against the building of yet more luxury (with some 'affordable') flats in her hometown. Her tea and cake friends had an easy job persuading her to put her name forward.

Despite it being the end of the week, the developers have agreed to meet locals to press their case, and the locals are certainly ready to press theirs. With her husband not far behind, Sarah is leading the charge.

After Alice left six years ago, Sarah's board appointed another CEO, but things didn't work out that well and he left a couple of years later. It was said that there had been 'some turbulence'.

One of the newer board members spotted the obvious pattern. But this pattern was not so obvious to Sarah the founder, who had got upset and left. It hadn't been easy for her, nor indeed for anyone. A hard time followed but, despite damaged reputation and funding struggles, the charity survived for a few years and then merged with (actually was taken over by) a much bigger national organization.

Sometimes we might lift up the path from behind us, put it in front of us and then travel along it. We think we are moving forward when actually we are not seeing a new path but simply re-enacting our old one.

Bob

Waiting for other committee members to land around the table, Bob helps himself to coffee (black, sweet) and a biscuit. Bob prefers meetings in person, saying, 'Three dimensions are a lot better than two.' He thinks, *Not a bad way to spend a Friday morning.*

The previous year, Daniel had recommended him to the powers that be as a member of a national advisory group on youth crime and gangs. Despite his mounting cynicism about there being more talk than action, Bob is enjoying it well enough. Apart from anything else it gives him exposure, which now lands him gigs as a keynote speaker.

'And get this,' he said to his wife. 'You know that soap you watch every day? Well, they've got a storyline coming up about some kids doing bad stuff and they've asked me to be an advisor. I was at the TV studio the other day and bumped into that Rose I told you about, you know, the arty one with pink hair that I met at that conference when the fire alarm went off and we all ended up on the street.'

Bob's dream is coming true. He had always wanted to write and be creative and is chuffed to bits to be graduating from being a big fish in a little pond to being a little fish in a much bigger pond. He entertains a fantasy that one day he will make it to being a big fish in a big pond. Time will tell.

Having each managed to rise beyond their egos, Bob and Daniel continued to be a 'dynamic duo' over several more years. They had started with meeting weekly in person and then settled on fortnightly, then online and then monthly as things settled. They developed a way of working that got them through the inevitable tricky times as they popped up. Quite different characters, they had managed to maintain trust, which they built by shared commitment to the cause, lots of patience, perseverance and doing their best to forgive as and when necessary.

Having completed three terms of three years of service, Daniel knew it was high time to announce his retirement. After an external recruitment process, the board, who had asked for Bob's comments on their top two candidates, just the previous day had told him which candidate they had chosen.

She isn't Bob's preferred choice, but he can live with it. He wonders whether he has the energy to handle a change at the top after these seven years.

Is this my seven-year itch? he wonders. Part of him is up for the challenge, but he has also started thinking that it's time to scratch the itch. With his wife working in the local authority, they have enough cash to get them through. If not now, when?

'Good morning Bob,' says the Committee Chair as she enters the room. 'What are you getting up to these days?'

'Oh well, that's another story,' says Bob with a twinkle in his eye.
'Fancy one of these biscuits?'

Daniel

With a few dings of a wine glass, the room falls quiet. Daniel rises to his feet to make his farewell speech. He's in no doubt that his time has come, not only because he has served for nine years, but also because he feels in his bones that it's time to take it easy.

Having retired from full-time work, he has been feeling his interests shifting and his energy slowing; his body is also sending him messages that the time is coming for him to slow down. His regular grandad duties give him quite enough exercise, thank you very much.

'Thank you all for coming,' he starts. The room smiles at him, glass in one hand, a vol-au-vent in the other. He speaks fondly of his time at the helm of the charity and of his affection for those with whom he has shared the journey: 'It's not always been easy – we've had our moments, haven't we?' This draws knowing looks from around the room. Bob just smiles warmly.

Rose

Over large glasses of chardonnay, Rose and her friend look back on their mountain adventure and remember how they had spilled their distress loudly onto the slopes. They had raged, they had laughed, they had cried. It had worked.

After what felt like wandering in the wilderness, Rose had drawn a firm decisive line under her 24 years and had boldly launched herself into a new phase of life. After three months they had both come back refreshed, relieved and ready to start again.

Rose, ever the artist, rekindled her lifelong passion for drawing and found she was rather good at it. She drew grown-up's cats and dogs for money, children's hamsters for free and volunteered once a week, running sessions for adults with learning disabilities.

Shakespeare said that mercy 'blesseth him that gives and him that takes'.[21] Volunteering is like that too. It blesses the giver and the receiver. Especially as part of recovery from crisis, freely giving our time to serve other people is healing.

The word got round, Rose's niche business of drawing flourished and she soon progressed to horses. Horse owners, she discovered, had as much cash in the bank as affection for their animals, and their money and her passion took her all around the country – a nice little earner. She was even hired to advise a TV arts programme. Rubbing shoulders with the rich and famous wasn't really her thing, but she was intrigued to see how the other side lived, so she parked her rebellious nature.

Inspired by her autistic grandson whose creative gifts are many but who even at his young age is struggling with everyday tasks, she's now Chair of the local Parent Carer Forum, which makes sure the needs of children with special educational needs and disabilities are understood by decision-makers.

---

[21] William Shakespeare *The Merchant of Venice* Act IV, Scene I.

Looking back, sometimes she feels as if it was only yesterday, and at other times like she might have dreamed the whole painful episode of leaving behind the beloved community arts projects she had given birth to. But with the benefit of hindsight she tells her friends that the painful departure from her arts project was one of the best things to happen to her.

'You've left your frogginess behind,' said her friend, 'always jumping from one thing to another. You seem happy where you've landed.'

'Better frogless than legless,' chuckled Rose, recalling her energetic past.

An eye-opener and an ear-opener, the whole bruising experience had stopped her in her tracks and had woken her up to what she already knew. She had to make a change. 'Hmm, a joyful breakdown,' she mused with a wry smile.

She had waved farewell to her career in the voluntary sector, but her passion for the creative arts lives on.

Alice (she/her)

The sounds, the posters, the people and everything are brighter than they were eight hours earlier. Alice, her wife and their daughter are excited to be back home. Alice wasn't superstitious and had cunningly chosen to fly on Friday 13th because she had heard that there's more space.

After three interim CEO jobs, Alice was keen to see what life would be like outside the relative safety of the UK, and a silver lining appeared (with no cloud) when her partner got a short-term job opportunity in Boston. They took the chance and went. Their new way of life was exciting and unsettling in equal measure, and they loved it.

The short term became longer term but after a while they decided they'd had enough adventure and elected to follow their own sun and return home.

Alice was an energetic networker and got lucky. An old friend now teaching at the local college had asked if she had any time to prepare some training materials for a new course on community organizing. 'Yes, sure I'm up for that,' said Alice.

She had also put her name forward as a trustee of an innovative local charity doing social prescribing. Not only that but she would have a crack at local radio, as she had always fancied being on the airwaves. Her friends said Alice was 'on it' and always had been. She got through by being stubbornly optimistic, which helped her keep going when she thought about impending climate breakdown and ever more turbulent times ahead. *Endnote²⁸*

Now back in the comfort of their home, Alice switches on the coffee machine from her old team, still making those reassuring swooshing noises these six years later.

'Her intentions were good,' Alice had said to her wife, referring to former Chair Sarah, 'but she didn't get us, did she? But, you know, I think she had a heart of gold. It's okay.'

It may be that we are on the receiving end of the difficulties some people have in accepting our style of life and they may say the 'wrong' thing. If you think they have good intentions, consider the possibility of giving them the benefit of the doubt (and also know it's okay to challenge them).

Alice readily forgave, and her first-time CEO experience felt far behind her. 'Just a blip on the screen and fading,' she said.

Imran

She scans the rows of badges and deftly picks one out. 'Here it is, "Imran". Welcome. Cloakroom's over there, hot drinks through those doors – yes, getting cold outside isn't it – and main room is up the stairs. Speakers' desk is over there, down the corridor on the left. Opening plenary starts in 20 minutes.'

Brisk, courteous, to the point.

Imran feels strangely at home; strange when he thinks of the journey he has been on since bumping into the conference crowds and the *Big Issue* seller in that autumnal street those long seven years ago. Apparently insignificant at the time, that moment turned out to be a fork in his road.

Trustee, then Interim Chair, then Chair of a heritage charity and now trustee of a Community Interest Company and honorary treasurer of a social enterprise, he has landed in a good place. It suits him. It has been a rocky road sometimes, but he has ridden the bumps.

On his way to the speakers' desk, he's greeted warmly and often. His reputation has been growing and today he will present at a breakout session. He wonders if next year he will make it to the main stage.

Sharp, charming, humble, yet ambitious for himself and the communities he serves, Imran's investments are paying off.

Epilogue: Integrating (life goes on)

Each of the fictional characters in the wild waters story survived and found their way through. Their fictional stories are a composite of real stories of the hundreds of leaders I have been alongside over decades as group process facilitator and crisis coach.

All this and my own wild water experiences helped create my way of working and how I have gone about writing this book.

I don't want to go back into the real wild waters of Eswatini in Africa – once a lifetime is quite enough, thank you very much. Nor do I want to fall so deeply in those life wild waters again. Close behind that is my impulse to make good use of my learning, which I find is not only of benefit to other people but is also a vehicle for solidifying the after-wild-waters person I am and am becoming.

I have found too that people whom I have coached also have an impulse to pass on learning from their pain. Nervously (I didn't want to retraumatize), while writing this book, I mailed a number of former coaching clients asking if they might be willing to pass on something of their own experience. To my relief they said an unequivocal yes.

Not only did they say yes, but I also noticed that when I spoke with former coaching clients, they were keen to talk with me. 'I haven't really thought about this for ages,' and then followed an outpouring of recollections, redolent of the very first gushing conversation. There was still an energy in it; although cloudy waters had cleared, the mud that had sunk to the bottom could still be stirred.

At the time of writing, each has had the time to reflect, digest and, to a large extent, been able to integrate their experiences. Following the fictional stories in the first four chapters, Chapter 5 offers nuggets of learning from real-life charity CEOs who want others to benefit from their experiences.

When you were in the middle of crisis, the wild waters overwhelmed you. Some years later things look different. Looking back you will come to see your struggles as one bumpy professional moment in a long career, fading in the rear-view mirror.

Chapter 5
PASSING IT ON – 'MONDAYS'

*Twelve real leaders anonymously pass on their
learning and wisdoms from before, during and after
their own real wild waters experiences.*

These anonymous contributions are presented as being on a 'Monday', the start of a new week, symbolizing that contributors are passing on what they have learned and how their wild waters experiences have opened new chapters.

Most have been written by me following interview and edited by the contributor, and some were written by the contributor and edited by me. All have been approved for publication.

They are presented here in order of the wild waters phase they most strongly relate to, namely before, during, soon after and some years later.

Value your support network

Being a CEO can be enormously satisfying, particularly when you are shaping strategy and empowering staff of your organization. But, even if you have a good management team and supportive board, it can be an incredibly lonely job when you have to make difficult choices.

If you don't have a supportive board or a good management team, then the job becomes much harder as the challenge of advancing the mandate of the organization may get entangled with conflicts of interests and divergent understandings of respective roles.

Your Chair may not be able to empathize with the sorts of challenges that you uniquely face, perhaps because they haven't been a CEO themselves, and while some may realize their limitations and try to learn, others will not.

And your friends may not be able to offer the sort of consistent empathetic support you need to negotiate your difficulties.

So don't make your life harder than it has to be: make sure that you have a support network in place beyond the workplace, in your social and familial networks. This may be a professional association (ACEVO in the UK, for example) or other CEOs with whom you can discuss the issues you are facing and benefit from the insights of other leaders.

Importantly, don't be passive in your engagement with this support network, but actively nourish it. Meet with it. Ask questions. Ask for help. Offer advice. Offer empathy.

Although everything may be plain sailing to start with, know that there will be storms as you try to change the world for the better. That's when you will really need and value your support network... or feel its absence if you haven't put it in place and nourished it.

Look beyond your day job

Yes, your primary focus is your day job, but there's nothing to stop you looking beyond. With the knowledge and agreement of others and as long as you maintain a healthy balance, you might like to consider the possibility of creating a portfolio of roles to run alongside your day job. The extra effort would be well worth it.

For example, you might take on one or two non-executive director roles (paid), set out to build a reputation as a speaker or as a contributor for third sector printed and online media. Or, if you're sure you're not overdoing it, you might take on the responsibility of being a trustee or Chair of another charity.

Keeping your eyes wide open and looking beyond may well help you do your day job. Not only that, but it may also help to keep you 'in the game' when, for whatever reason, it's time to leave. Win win.

Act on your instinct and catch the moment

It could have worked out so differently. If, at that moment, I had insisted that the board paused and followed a wider recruitment process, maybe I wouldn't have gone through two years of massive struggle. I survived, albeit with bruises. Our dear organization survived too, albeit having suffered a major setback with the impact being felt at all levels of the organization.

I look back to that significant moment. That moment was when, after many years, it was time for our much-appreciated Chair to retire and several long-serving trustees were dealing with personal matters. The board had a decision to make. One of the recently appointed trustees put their hand up and gave a convincing sales pitch to a board consisting of mostly new trustees (both to the charity and the role of a trustee). The vote was passed and there was a momentary feeling of relief from the board, but in my gut a feeling of dread.

In that moment they had taken the line of least resistance. So had I; I felt powerless with no one to turn to. If only I had acted on my instincts. I knew then that I should have insisted that trustees stop and think, but I didn't say anything because I felt no one would listen to me.

From that moment there followed a couple of years during which I and the organization were more or less teetering on the brink of collapse. Then, after the sudden departure of the new Chair and two acting Chairs, the board instigated a thorough external recruitment process and involved me in it. Eventually they stepped up and we now have an excellent Chair at the helm. We are all looking ahead, and I am looking back to the moment when we might have chosen a less perilous path.

This drama was bigger than all of us

I thought it was all me,

But I just played my part.

I thought it was all me,

But there were others in the room.

I thought it was all me,

But our drama was bigger than all of us.

And none of us noticed.

With just one CEO before me, the founder, ours was quite a short organizational history. Nevertheless, it weighed heavily on me. After me there was another CEO. They too found it heavy and, like me, they left unhappily. Then came another, who is still struggling under the same weight of history.

So remember this: as a leader you inherit the joys and sorrows of the past. They may be a warm breeze at your back – lucky you. Or they may be boulders in your backpack.

I assumed what came to pass was all my failing, so I battled harder. If only I had seen that, yes, I played my part, but I was playing my part in a much bigger drama. Then I might, just might, have helped us see the source of the struggles that were shaping us all, and perhaps we may have been able to face our past and move on together.

Follow your gut instinct

My board had made a decision to start closing the charity. Three months after I completed all the redundancy consultations, I hit a low point and I remember telling my board that the stress was too much and I couldn't continue…

It was at that pivotal moment that I decided to follow my gut instinct.

My guts told me that despite all the negativity and crap that I was getting from the staff, it was the highest good for everybody that I stay in place as the CEO. I knew this was the best way to bring the organization to a smooth and orderly closure and, in the long term, that it would be best for me too.

That decision definitely caused me a lot of discomfort and soon after I finally closed the door on the organization I got a nasty dose of shingles, which knocked me out for several months.

But I look at my life now, and the decisions I have made since that pivotal moment five years ago by always following my gut instincts. I see that my life is so much better now. I have retired, divorced (and have a new partner), a new home. Life is very different and much better.

Shame – name it and move beyond

The issue I was managing felt like an attack on who I was. It reached my very core, my heart and the essence of my being, making me question everything.

I couldn't deal with the issue because I couldn't name it, because of how shameful that would be. In retrospect I waited too long before talking with someone.

When I finally sought support, the subsequent conversations helped me to understand that the issue was not a personal indictment, although it felt that way. I realized that as a Chief Executive and a person I can be vulnerable and mess up and get stuck, despite trying really hard.

With the knowledge that, with help, I can move above and beyond shame and other deeply personal feelings, I will be more resilient and better prepared if and when these personal challenges come up in future.

Take your own standing-eight count

My head was pounding. My ribs ached. There was blood coming from my nose. As a boxer, I did exactly what I was trained to do in the ring. Take an eight count. Breathe again. Focus. Make a clear decision to carry on. Guard up, chin down, steady legs, come back fighting...

Workwise, my eight seconds lasted three months, and when I was in the middle of those three months they lasted a lifetime.

But eventually the board stepped up and did the right thing. They did right by telling the Chair that their behaviour had been unacceptable and that the charity had come perilously close to collapse. The Chair had meant well but had appeared to have little or no insight into the impact of their daily micromanagement.

It was tough for me – so tough that I was on sick leave for three months. It was my very own 'eight count'.

In boxing, if a fighter is knocked down, the referee has to give an eight count for the fighter to refocus and recover before making a judgement call about whether or not the fight can safely continue.

This analogy helped me during the cold, dark days of being down and nearly-but-not-quite out. When I was down, the board – the 'referee' – was looking the other way, so as an amateur boxer I gave myself an eight count. When I eventually returned to work, the board woke up to what was happening and knew that they needed to make a judgement call. They did: the Chair left, I stayed.

This is where the analogy breaks down a bit. Now I'm not fighting but am managing a successful organization that's looking back on its near-death experience and is going from strength to strength. The board, the staff and the CEO are working, training and winning together. The last board meeting was our most successful ever; we are back in the game!

Hold firm

Our organization was well run and successful. Nevertheless, it seemed that they were out to get me.

There was an orchestrated campaign from some corners of our network to undermine the national organization. Some trustees, put there by their regions, were busying themselves arguing for their regional, not our shared national interests.

I was in the frontline and it was getting personal (although I was told it wasn't!). I faced it with all the courage I could muster and did what came naturally – and what came naturally turned out to be pretty effective.

I only shared some of the problem with my staff team, so they were confident that I was on top of things and believed in what we were doing, so they could concentrate on doing their jobs. Thinking they might no longer invest in us, I didn't tell a soul outside about our troubles within. I kept my mouth shut when I needed to.

I got support from outside our organization to keep my feet on the ground and to make sense of what was happening.

To dispel growing myths about our performance, I arranged an independent external inspection – which told me what I knew, namely that, contrary to the criticisms, we were doing well. We made a new strategic plan and, although it sat on the shelf, it was enough to concentrate minds.

I fully expected the madness to conclude with the organization being ripped apart. The damage to me personally was immense, but holding firm saved the organization and we went on to become financially secure with a big reputation. I continued in post for another seven years until I retired, passing on a well-funded organization.

Journeying through the river of grief

I had to leave a job that I loved. It was a bereavement. It hurt. Sometimes, when I see other charity CEOs, I have feelings of envy about what an amazingly privileged job I did and that they are still doing.

For a long time, moments of grief came over me, but I noticed that they were slowly becoming less upsetting and further apart. I took myself by the hand and discovered ways to help me heal. I found that being in nature and wide-open spaces, close to home and also far away, really helped me to accept what had happened.

After a while the tears became less frequent (I had often wondered if it had all been too much for my friends, but they stayed with me). My self-confidence returned, I came to see what happened many years ago in a broader perspective, and I have found new ways of expressing my impulse to be of service to other people.

Grateful every day

After my tribunal success, exposing damaging behaviours within the charity I worked for, I felt exhausted, not triumphant. Despite attempts at other CEO roles, the betrayal left me disheartened. Communication became a struggle; emails and calls triggered fear. With no job, money or former colleagues, I stumbled into an unexpected career shift – becoming a painter and decorator. Prompted by personal challenges, I found solace in the simplicity of this new path, discovering a sense of accomplishment even in its modest beginnings.

From the instant gratification of bringing smiles through my painting, I ventured into entrepreneurship, building a respected business over five years. Beyond paint, I delve into my clients' lives, forming connections that transcend walls.

Specializing in work with people with disabilities and dementia, I have become a social prescriber of sorts. My creative journey unexpectedly led me to product promotional work, even appearing in adverts for well-known brands.

No longer burdened by shame or stress, I have embraced a balanced, fulfilling life where creativity and family take precedence. With a supportive partner and a newfound sense of control, I have moved positively beyond my past career, prioritizing family and personal fulfilment.

Content with my career and accepted in a male-dominated industry, I have found fulfilment and respect. Reflecting on the tribunal, I view it as a valuable learning experience. My advice to CEOs, directors and trustees is to establish a professional support network early. Seek external guidance to navigate challenges, fostering a team to discuss concerns and formulate responses earlier. Hindsight, in my case, highlighted the importance of timely support, a lesson I'm grateful for every day.

Be a (super) human, not a superhuman

It took me five years to discover what I knew all along.

I held on for three long years of the seven in one job, locked in battle with elements on the board whose vested interest in the status quo was holding back modernization of the charity's governance. This was followed immediately by two full years in another demanding CEO role that included steering that charity through the Covid-19 pandemic. After those five draining years, I finally chose to take one year for myself and discovered an obvious truth.

During those five years that I was running, fighting and struggling, my energy tank was draining. Drop by drop, every day. Anger, pig-headed determination, a stiff upper lip, my karate training and knowing that the charity, seen from the outside, was flourishing all drove me on. On top of that I was supercharged by the certain knowledge that my advice to trustees, who were not listening, was correct; this was worth fighting for, but fighting drained me.

Having finally admitted defeat/seen sense I hung on until I could move on at a time of my choosing. I found to my great relief that my new board did listen and was a pleasure to work with. The mission of the charity was close to my heart. All was well – until I realized that I couldn't find the resolve and resilience I needed to deal with inevitable management challenges that came my way. Yes, outside me was better, but inside me was not.

Then I chose a year of calming, digestion and recovery. I took a year out of the workplace in order to focus on physical, mental and emotional healing. Money was tight, but it was so worth it. No regrets. I have found a new way of working, know that I'm a human who needs to take care of energy reserves and have discovered the obvious truth that I'm definitely not a superhuman.

My prisoner lived rent-free in my head then after walking 1,000 miles, I forgave

My prisoner was my hurt, my anger, the sense of injustice of it all. What happened to me was unjust. I had done nothing wrong, but they told me I had. How could they!?

My leaving day arrived with no thank you, no party and no closure. Not even a card to say goodbye after eight years in the job.

This pain I carried for way too long. Then one day my caring vicar said to me: 'When you don't forgive someone, you allow them to live rent-free in your head. Is that how you want to live your life?'

Taking myself in hand, I set off on the Camino de Santiago. I had never walked anywhere but it seemed that I had nothing to lose. After six weeks of walking, sharing and reflecting, I found myself back at home, still carrying my 'prisoner'.

Then I realized that *I'm not done yet*. So I packed my bag again, got myself a better pair of walking shoes and set off for the Camino del Norte this time.

And slowly I was able to leave my hurt behind, as I walked the beautiful green hills of northern Spain, day after day.

With that forgiveness I was able to open a new chapter in my life. Wishing to 'end well', I embarked on a fast-track training towards ordination as a priest in the Church of England.

My lifelong vocation of service as a 'servant leader' continues and is gaining expression in a new form. The headspace occupied for so long by my 'prisoner' is now being enriched by the intricacies of how to help people through illness, births, deaths, marriages and the life transitions and pains that will certainly come their way.

ACKNOWLEDGEMENTS

Writing a book is a lonely business. Except when it isn't – 96% (a made-up figure, but it feels about right) of the time I have been alone, creating, writing, worrying, deleting, rewriting, restructuring. The other 4% of the time I have been supported along the way by a host of fellow travellers. It's that combined 100% that has delivered this book.

I can't imagine that I would have seen this venture through without the steadfast, warm, insightful encouragement and support of Jenny Berry, Support Advisor at ACEVO. She consistently told me that the effort was worthwhile, commented on multiple manuscripts and convinced me that the book would, one day, be serving leaders before, during and after crisis.

I wouldn't have started in the first place had it not been for Debbie Bannigan, who in London at 12.15 on 20 October 2016 told me firmly that I had to share my experience of crisis coaching and facilitation. Her early analysis and my own interviews helped me to make sense of charity leaders' experiences and gave me the impetus to start writing.

A massive thank you to Marianne Hartley (Hartley & Soul) for page designs, consistent encouragement and for her magnificent book cover design.

Special thanks to Sir Nick Young, whose early endorsement lifted me out of despair and inspired me to continue; his foreword is at the beginning of this book.

Amanda Falkson's comments and certainty that the book would be of service, together with early encouragement from Vicky Browning, Stefan Kuchar and Hélène Frost, kept me paddling ahead.

Readers who offered comments on draft manuscripts, which were often difficult to swallow but always on the button, propelled me from what I now see was an inadequate first manuscript to a sixth: Maryanne Matthews, Lainya Offside-Keivani, Gail Scott-Spicer, Ros Spearing, Linda Laurance, Alastair Pettigrew, Leah Antignas, Gareth Oughton, Karina Luchinkina, Rosanna Farrell, Alistair Griggs, Bernd Eiden and Greg Dalder, especially those last-named who offered comments on multiple manuscripts.

I appreciate the fortitude of many hundreds of leaders in the UK and internationally over more than two decades who have allowed me to help them navigate their individual and group wild waters. By my helping them, they have helped me become a better coach and facilitator.

I particularly thank the CEOs who, in Chapter 5, willingly accepted my invitation to anonymously contribute their learning about their crisis times to benefit other good leaders.

I offer my thanks to Browns, Kingston upon Thames and Hollyhock café, Richmond, whose river views and ambiance provided ideal containers for my many ponderings. Also, last but not least, massive appreciation to everyone at Practical Inspiration Publishing and especially founder and director Alison Jones, who generously spotted the hidden potential of my first manuscript. Without her and her colleagues' energetic guidance, I would still be wading through the swamp.

MY LIVING AND WORKING ASSUMPTIONS

I do my best to live my life and do my coaching and facilitation work on the assumption that the following principles are true. I hope stating them here helps you to understand where I'm coming from.

- Suffering is an inherent part of the human condition and that sometimes our suffering becomes overwhelming is virtually inevitable.
- By understanding the causes of suffering we can find a way through it.
- It's possible for each of us to recover from bad things that we experience and, as we learn how to suffer, we suffer less.
- We are not alone and everything on Earth and beyond is connected. So what I do or do not do will influence other people, other living things and everything.
- Beyond our apparent differences such as age, gender, ability, race, class, heritage, sexual orientation, culture, stage in life, we are all equal.
- I and we all construct perceptions (mental formations) that if untrue can trigger inappropriate and unhelpful responses.
- Each one of us is able to choose how we respond to the actions of others.
- My life experience influences so far create my experiences today.
- My life is influenced by the lives of my familial and cultural ancestors.
- Deep listening with no interruption has powerful healing potential.
- Being fully present with and sensing what's happening and may emerge is a powerful way of helping.

- Sometimes I and we can and do fail to live in line with our principles and we can seek to put things right when that happens.
- Discovering and doing what's now mine to do, the calling of my best self, is my most intelligent response to the turbulent times I and we all are living through.

THE AUTHOR

As a teenager, thinking about the meaning of life and noticing injustices and bad things happening, I felt a strong impulse to make the world a better place. (I know, that's not unusual.)

Now at the 'retiring' end of a career of six decades working with, in and alongside civil society organizations, I find that my impulse lives on. As befits the age and *my* age, that impulse is now finding a new form; my creating this book is one expression of that.

My training in body psychotherapy in London in the 1970s and 80s was to become an underpinning for my career in many community settings and large organizations such as Save the Children and the British Red Cross.

At the turn of the millennium the wild waters of redundancy and unplanned departures propelled me into establishing get2thepoint to coach leaders and facilitate groups to help them to find clarity and move forward. I have worked with many hundreds of civil society organizations in the UK and, since 2002, with the UN and other international bodies.

Since serving as Director for Europe, Middle East, North Africa, on the global board of the International Association of Facilitators (IAF) for three years from 2013, my practice has grown and so have I. In 2022 I was awarded Certified Professional Facilitator | Emeritus status by the IAF.

Having learned about the vicissitudes of organizational dynamics from close up, I have acquired a solid understanding of leadership and organizational systems. My experience of the transformative power of 'generative attention' in my own coaching sessions with Nancy Kline over 14 years, and the teachings of Thích Nhất Hạnh, have become bed rocks of my practice.

My wife and my grown-up son and daughter have been alongside me through thick and thin, navigating the excitements, joys, sorrows and upsets of my attempts to live a decent life.

After six decades of leading, managing, facilitating, coaching, I have stepped back from the active frontline to create this book, hoping that it will serve the leaders who are still there.

Martin Farrell
29 May 2024
www.get2thepoint.org

RESOURCES

In addition to whatever you may have found in this book, you have many resources available to you to help navigate wild waters. They serve you as you take a breather from your struggle, regain strength and renew perspective: a walk in nature alone or with someone close to you, sharing with a friend in a warm café, professional help from a therapist, coach, a mentor, doctor, alternative medical practitioner, online or in-person spiritual communities, nourishing food, running, fresh air, music, books, journals, podcasts, and more and more...

Now you have some more. A growing library of resources is freely available for you. When you see *Endnotes* go to www.martinfarrell. org/good-leaders-help

Endnotes

Introduction
1 Leadership qualities
2 Leadership competencies
3 Noble truths

Chapter 1
4 Two wolves
5 Presencing
6 Listening

INDEX

References to footnotes show both the page number and the note number (e.g. 200n19).